F

To

Heaven

From Here
To
Heaven

Tom Walker

HODDER AND STOUGHTON
LONDON SYDNEY AUCKLAND TORONTO

British Library Cataloguing in Publication Data

Walker, Tom
   From here to heaven.—(Hodder Christian paperbacks).
   1. Christian life
   I. Title
   248.4   BV4501.2

   ISBN 0 340 42352 8

Contents

Preface

In his classic book *Pilgrim's Progress*, John Bunyan described the hazardous journey that a Christian makes in travelling from here to heaven. There are many temptations on the way, crises of guidance, traumas of illness and bereavement, as a Christian comes to terms with living together with God in a world of suffering and imperfection.

This book speaks from personal experience and is meant to help those who have begun to follow the call of Jesus Christ, God's Son. It is anecdotal rather than autobiographical, and illustrates from experience how God's love and grace can be manifested in any Christian's pilgrimage.

When I first began to follow Christ, I was immensely helped by books which described how other Christians coped with failure and doubt in their lives, as well as with achievement and success in walking with God. I hope this book shares the joys of discovering the healing and forgiveness that Jesus Christ has won for us on the cross, and testifies to the power of his resurrection in a Christian's experience. In it the new believer should find encouragement and the seeker after truth may find hope.

Tom Walker

1 The smiling face of God

A party of Scouts, rucksacks on back, stood gazing fascinatedly at the steaming, puffing monster that had pulled a trainload of trippers the easy way to the summit of Snowdon. It was a bright day with gleams of sunlight piercing through the clouds. The usual haze and mist of the cloud-capped peak had disappeared, and the most glorious views were to be seen in every direction. Small lakes glistened at the foot of steep hills, fed by tiny streams that looked no more significant than a scribbled pencil line drawn haphazardly on a giant relief map.

'Let's get going,' the leader called, and the Scouts scurried together, ready to make an easy descent to their camp site on the lower mountain slopes, just near the little town of Llanberis. 'Keep near the railway track so that we don't get lost.'

Despite having maps and compasses and knowing the area quite well the patrol leader was taking no chances. He had been asked to see the younger boys safely back to camp, and he was in no mood for heroics on the mountainside.

And well he might be careful.

Within a very few minutes of starting off, the clouds suddenly descended and the mountain top with its ugly restaurant and puffing-billy train was lost from view. It was quickly too dark to read either map or compass and a fierce wind blew the young Scouts inexorably across the railway track towards the sheer drop down into the Llanberis Pass, hundreds of feet below. 'Lie down – flat on your faces – get down now,' the leader shouted, and with heart thumping against the hard ground each Scout lay motionless. It seemed an age, but as suddenly as it had started the wind dropped and the cloud cleared, and sunshine broke through again. It was soon safe for the boys to stand upright. But not without a clutch of fear in their hearts as each one saw that they had been blown to within a few inches of the sheer drop to the valley below.

I was the leader of that patrol, and looking back I can remember a definite sense of thanksgiving for protection. I did not know how to say thank you through Jesus Christ, but the whole incident spoke to me of an over-ruling purpose of love which I could only later attribute to the providence of God. The thoughts that actually ran through my mind were immensely selfish: 'Supposing I had died, where would I have gone?' But I was even more bothered about how I would have lived with the feeling of responsibility for another boy's death. I could not see how I would ever again have slept well in my bed. Indeed, although I had no sure faith in the promise of life after death, I would rather have died myself than live with a conscience burdened by that kind of responsibility.

Our startling and frightening experience had wonder-fully focused my mind on the major issues of life and death. The problem was, at that stage I had no idea there was a smiling face behind the apparently 'frowning providence'. My primitive and untaught views of God tied in with Thomas Hardy's assessment. He was only

> that dreaming, dumb, dark thing
> That turns the handle of this idle show.

Without any sense of God being personally interested in me or in anyone else, I could not imagine a loving purpose behind the stories of tragic death in a world of accident, chance and unconquered disease. Our brush with near disaster weighed heavily on my mind.

However, as we trudged thankfully towards the camp site at the foot of Snowdon the enthusiastic singing of Scout songs soon made us put the fear out of our minds. Embryonic thoughts of the meaning of life, death and eternal reality came to nothing. 'She'll be coming round the mountain when she comes' quickly shut out all thoughts of God.

But God has a way of breaking into our apathy. It was only a day after we nearly fell off the edge of Mount Snowdon that we were again caught by the vicissitudes of the Welsh weather. We were camping in a steeply sloping field, with our ex-army bell tents scattered here and there on the flattest pieces of ground. Right in the centre stood a massive marquee containing tables and benches for corporate meals. Near to each tent was an open fire for the patrol cooking, but many of the main meals were prepared on Calor Gas stoves inside the marquee itself. It poured with rain almost every day, and gradually the whole field became like a broad river bed as torrents of water poured from the hillside. Deep trenches were dug around the tents, but as the ground became more sodden and the winds grew stronger there was increasing anxiety about the security of the camp.

Then one day at tea-time the moment of drama came. I was in our patrol tent at the very bottom of the field, feeling unwell and unable to eat. Everyone else was tucking into a meal in the marquee; the storm that day had come to its peak, and rain was pounding on the canvas roofs and the guy-ropes were straining in a fierce wind. Suddenly there was a loud rending sound and a tremendous shout went up from the marquee. I dashed to the doorway of the tent and looked up the hill to see the huge marquee collapsing to the ground. It was like some slow-motion TV repeat of an incident in a sporting spectacular. I grabbed my boots and forced my way against the driving storm as quickly as I could. There were urgent shouts for help and, aware of the massive size of the central poles, I feared that somebody might have been crushed beneath them. The risk of fire spreading from the cooking stoves was also not to be ignored, despite the smothering effect of the wet canvas.

Mercifully not a single person was seriously hurt, and although it was impossible even to sort out what damage had been done until better weather returned, each patrol of bedraggled Scouts bedded down for the night in their double-guyed and double-checked tents, hoping that they would remain standing until the morning.

I did not know much about the life of John Wesley at that time, but he once had a near escape from death when his father's house caught fire and as a small child he was rescued from the flames. He often referred to himself as 'a brand plucked from the burning' and I similarly felt singled out by a protecting purpose. I could not understand that it was the hand of God, but twisting and turning uncomfortably in my sodden sleeping bag that night, I could not help reflecting on the events of the day. Isolated from all the others, and an observer of another near-disaster, I felt singularly aware of being spoken to. By whom I knew not. God was not personal or close. I had no reason to be favoured. Others died tragically in mountain-top ventures and others were killed or injured in unforeseen accidents. Twice I felt I had been miraculously preserved in as many days.

The trouble with learning lessons from human experience is that so often 'I' am at the centre of the stage. Everything seems to revolve around 'me', and I am more conscious of my needs than I am of the living God speaking to me. But where else are we to start? God always starts where we are, which is why Jesus his Son came to be born as a human being, in order to meet us in our circumstances and on our wavelength. Although I was a long way from relating any of these happenings to an experience of Jesus, that camp was undoubtedly a time when God was breaking through the crust of my adolescent selfishness to say, 'I am real, I do love you, and I will look after you.' I was still saying to God, 'Who are you? Is there an answer to my questions? How do I find reality in my religion?'

2 Pale beginnings

I learnt my first lesson about physics the hard way. I was still in the kindergarten, finding out what a big and wonderful world we live in. On the way to school one freezing winter's morning I was amazed to see the giant icicles hanging down from metal railings, like huge, cornet-shaped ice lollies just waiting to be licked. I broke off as many as I could and carried them to school. They showed no sign of thawing, so I did what seemed to be the sensible thing. I popped them in my Wellington boots so that I could take them home to Mum when school was over. Imagine my surprise, after the last lesson was over and I went to the cloakroom to get ready to go home, when I saw water seeping underneath the door. Imagine my horror when I paddled through a sizeable pool on the cloakroom floor, as I discovered that standing in the middle of this miniature flood were my own Wellington boots, brimful and overflowing with water! The icicles were nowhere to be seen.

We often learn truths about life and nature and creation long before we have formal instruction in practical science. So it is in God's school. The good providence of God is such that long before we come to our step of personal faith in Christ, he is drawing us to himself and breaking down the barriers that we have set up to keep us isolated from his love.

The dawning of truth is always gradual, and we grow up into the truth about him in much the same way as we grow up physically. Sometimes there are periods of steady but imperceptible growth, and sometimes there are lulls. A friend of mine became a Christian during his first term at university, and went home with great enthusiasm to share the good news with his mother that his life was now changed. As far as she was concerned he hadn't changed a bit. He thought he had taken a tremendous step in coming from his dim groping after God to a real and personal experience of Jesus Christ, but she had little evidence of growth as yet, and only as the months and years went by did she see that in fact the change was real and radical. He had become a new person in Christ Jesus, and was growing into his likeness.

Many people find, however, that although their thoughts have begun to turn to God (as mine did on Mount Snowdon) and they have started to attend a church and associate with other Christians, they still lack a specific moment of conversion to which they can look back. They hear their friends' talk about a personal faith and a living relationship with God through Jesus Christ, and they feel cheated because they have no dramatic turning point such as St Paul knew on the Damascus road, and to which so many Christians testify. This can be particularly true of those who grow up in a Christian home and from their earliest days have a habit of going to Sunday school and church.

In some parts of the world the dawning of day is sudden. One moment it is darkness and the next moment there is the light of a new day. Further away from the Equator the dawning of light is far more gradual as night moves through the dusky dawn to the pale beginnings of a new day's light. But when day has dawned anyone can say, 'I am in the daylight *now*; I can see.' Anyone who can say that about spiritual reality does not have to worry about the manner by which they've come into the light of Christ. They can simply rejoice in it.

Even when God touches our lives through vivid experiences we have no means of getting to know him. Take the case of the blind man in John 9. The transforming thing for him was that Jesus came to him. The

disciples wanted to argue about *why* the man was blind –
was it because of his own sin or his parents' sin? Jesus,
however, saw that he had been provided for the display
of a mighty work of God. He realised that after years of
being blind to the material world, quite apart from being
blind to the things of God, this man was ready to believe
and to be made a new person. 'I am the light of the
world,' Jesus had said (John 8:12; 9:5), and now it was as
though he was saying to this man in no uncertain terms,
'Let there be light in your eyes and in your heart.' After
Jesus anointed the man's eyes with clay and commanded
him to go and wash in the pool of Siloam, he obeyed and
'came back seeing' (John 9:7).

God can be working out his good purposes in our lives
while we continue in the darkness of unbelief. It was like
that for St Paul. We talk of his sudden conversion, but in
fact God was dealing with him long before the crisis
moment when he met Jesus on the Damascus road. He
was in the forefront of opposition to the preaching of the
gospel, and when Stephen, the first Christian martyr,
was stoned the witnesses laid down their garments at his
feet (Acts 7:58). At that time Saul (as he was then known)
'was ravaging the church, and entering house after
house, he dragged off men and women and committed
them to prison' (Acts 8:3). Indeed, he was 'still breathing
threats and murder against the disciples of the Lord'
(Acts 9:1) when he had his personal encounter with the
living Christ. Sometimes the clearest evidence that God is
dealing with us and drawing us to himself is that we
become increasingly angry and opposed to everything
that has to do with Christianity. Because of our spiritual
blindness, we are as helpless as the man who was born
blind, in that we are unable to see the truth about God.
We do blatantly wrong things, against our conscience,
without realising that we are hurting God in the process.
Saul thought he was persecuting Christians, but
Jesus said, 'Saul, Saul, why do you persecute me?'
(Acts 9:4).

As we grope around, quite unaware of how distant we are from God, a glimmer of the truth may break through from time to time. Without acknowledging the fullness of God's creative power we may be struck with the beauty of a sunset or a landscape or, like a small boy, be fascinated by the construction of an icicle. Without admitting to moral absolutes we may find ourselves with a bad conscience after doing something which we know to be wrong. Like Paul, we can even think we are serving God in a religious cause, and yet be far from doing his will. Certainly I needed more than a few frightening experiences to make me stop and think, especially when years of churchgoing had not brought God's light into my personal darkness. Just as the blind man needed Jesus to cross his path, and as Paul needed the light of Jesus Christ shining brighter than the noonday sun on that Damascus road, I needed Jesus to speak to me, to meet me, and to enlighten me. Having given the blind man his sight Jesus wanted him to come to a fuller understanding about himself and he asked if he believed in the Son of man. The man's answer was as vague as mine would have been when I was still searching for God – 'And who is he, sir, that I may believe in him?'. But now the blind man could see Jesus as the answer to his problem. His mind was informed as well as his sight restored, and Jesus said to him, 'You have seen him, and it is he who speaks to you.' He said, 'Lord, I believe,' and 'he worshipped him' (John 9:35–38).

So many people suggest that to believe in God is to take a step of blind faith. But this incident shows that we are in darkness already because of the sinfulness of our nature which prevents us from seeing God and following him. But when Jesus comes along as 'the light of the world' (John 9:5) we step out of darkness into the light that he brings to our scene. Dawn's pale beginning may not seem to be a very promising start to the brightness of a new day, but in the Christian life, as in our quest for more earthly knowledge, we start with a glimmer

11

of understanding and grow steadily until we can cope with the brightness of God's full revelation in Christ.

3 Trained reverence

Though I was blind to the things of God myself, I was not an irreligious person. I had acquired a 'trained reverence', to use Julian Huxley's phrase, though I completely lacked what he called 'discipline of the soul'. I was also, despite years of regular churchgoing from the age of six, a million miles away from any religion of personal salvation. The practice of churchgoing was simply part of my family's tradition. We chose to go to church, others did not. But it became a handicap in my personal search for God because I felt a constant hypocrite: there were so many things promised to the Christian disciple which were manifestly not true in my experience. If my defences were aroused, I was the first to claim my history of regular churchgoing in self justification. 'No one can say I'm not a Christian, I go to church five times a Sunday!'

The reason for such regular attendance was my absorbing interest in church music. I had intense loyalty to the fine parish church choir as I grew up in Dorking and I was the first to help at any extra services when I was old enough to play the organ.

One of the anthems I used to sing as a boy was William Boyce's 'O where shall wisdom be found?' This was based on words taken from the book of Ecclesiastes in the Old Testament, a book melancholy in tone, reflecting the emptiness of life without God. At the beginning of the twelfth chapter the writer says: 'Remember also your Creator in the days of your youth, before the evil days come, and the years draw nigh, when you will say, "I have no pleasure in them"'. The whole book is about the pursuit of wisdom, and I was as eager as I could be in pursuing wisdom. What I really needed was someone to come alongside and help me, because at that stage I was deeply impressionable concerning the things of God. Though still groping in the dark, I had not forgotten the sense of God's overruling intervention in the Scout camp experiences.

At that stage I did not get very much help at home. This was surprising because our churchgoing was regular and sincere, and there was a reality of true love in the family relationships. Nevertheless, Christian faith was never a topic of discussion. It was only later, after I had made the discovery of a personal relationship with Christ, that I rather unkindly challenged my father on this and accused him of prayerlessness and lack of instruction in the things of God. Initially he was greatly hurt by my accusations, but then confessed that because he had grown up in an earnest Strict Baptist family, he had had Christian religion thrust down his throat from his earliest childhood days.

Because the Strict Baptists in his town were quite a small group they tended to be aggressive towards other Christians who did not share all their dogmatic views, and the discovery during the Great War of Christians with broad sympathies (not to mention people of other, non-Christian faiths), caused my father to have severe doubts about the wisdom of indoctrinating his own children. Whereas his parents had always begun their meals with a spoken family grace, he gave up this practice lest it should smack of hypocrisy.

That is not to say that there was not a very genuine understanding of Christian ways, and indeed a living out of Christian standards at earlier stages of his life. (As a civil servant he was nicknamed 'the Bishop' by his colleagues because of his church adherence, and he took great delight in introducing himself to senior ecclesiastics whom he sometimes met in the course of his official duties as 'the Bishop of the London Postal Region', of which he was Staff Controller at the time.) His own earnest quest after God was pursued through lengthy discussions with a godly country rector who introduced him to the rather gentler and less crusading approach of rural Anglicanism. That in turn led him to a local parish church in Dorking where his musical interest was matched by the very fine standards of the church choir, and without any sinister rejection of the gospel he was *en route* for God.

What his parents could not show through hard dogmas, he was discovering slowly but definitely as God's hand was upon him. Indeed, the ultimate flowering of this personal faith came in his eighties as he shared his last years with us after my mother died. This was the first time since his boyhood that he had been able to worship regularly at a Bible-teaching church. He was stimulated to read the Bible with the help of commentaries as he spent many hours alone in his room. At the time when a large number of elderly people grow frustrated by their loss of mobility and experience of pain, my father blossomed in his knowledge of God. Before this happened, his restricted circumstances made his room seem like a prison-house. As he grew in faith, he discovered that it was not so much a prison as a nest – a place of security and a place for growth in his Christian understanding.

This is a salutary story for those of us who want instant results and a packaged perfection in our early years of searching for God. It is right for the Preacher to say, 'Remember also your Creator in the days of your youth', but we must remember that youthful doubts can take some time for God to penetrate. Although as young people we can be very open to the reality of God, the business of having our eyes opened is a matter for God's sovereign timing.

In the selfishness of my criticism of my parents I had not stopped to think that they had also been young once and had been open to God in the days of their youth. The fact that neither had found an informed personal faith in

15

their younger days was not through want of searching, so it was indeed harsh of me to judge their attitudes. In my immaturity I thought that to be truly born again every Christian should have an experience just like mine. I could not see that we were on a longer timescale, and I did not make allowance for the insecurities that the horrors of the First World War and the severe Depression in the 1930s brought to a generation which grew up with the tail end of Victorian super-confidence and Edwardian emancipation. We are all children of our time, and the climate and circumstances in which we grow up significantly affect our search after God.

In the gospel pages we find recorded a variety of experiences as men and women meet Jesus Christ. Peter and his partners had a thriving fishing business and they were given a straight word of command: 'Follow me' (Matt 4:19). We also know from John's gospel that Peter's first contact with Jesus came through an introduction made by his brother, who was himself so thrilled at meeting Jesus that he could not wait to introduce his own relatives and friends to him (John 1:40–42). Some, like the blind man of John 9, found that it was their handicap that introduced them to Jesus, when in God's good purpose he was in just the right place for a miracle; but in Mark 2:3–12 the paralysed man had to be brought by his friends and lowered through the flat-topped roof of a house in order to hear the words: 'Your sins are forgiven' (v. 5). His healing came because his friends had sufficient faith to believe that Jesus could solve his problem and were also loving enough to put themselves out to bring him right to the feet of Jesus.

Others went to great lengths to avoid making their interest in Jesus public. Zacchaeus, a corrupt tax collector and collaborator with the hated Romans, thought he would be unobserved by Jesus when he climbed into a tree (Luke 19:1–10), but none the less, as Jesus passed by with a huge crowd, he stopped and invited him down. Nicodemus the Pharisee showed how tentative his approach to Jesus was by coming to him under cover of the darkness (John 3) – a symbol of his own spiritual darkness and his need for a completely new start in life. For years he had sought to follow God according to the Old Testament code, and was a devout member of the Sanhedrin, the Jewish religious and legal council. But full enlightenment came only with his cautious approach to Jesus Christ personally.

Some had to be brought to an awareness of their sinfulness in God's sight before they could truly understand the claims of Christ. This was true of the woman whom Jesus met at the Samaritan well (John 4). As soon as he touched on her immorality she knew that there was pressure on her to decide which way her life should go. She tried to divert the matter by introducing some theological controversy – we too always drag up the dregs of our religious experience in order to counter the specific call of Christ to follow him – but soon she surrendered and was able to acknowledge him as Christ. Then she told her friends about him.

Each person came to Christ in their own personal and distinctive way, and the important thing was that they had found him – or rather that he had found them.

As I said earlier, during my schooldays I was looking for someone to come alongside and help me in my search for God. But no one I knew seemed to know any more about God than I did. We were a strangely unthinking bunch. We were taught to imbibe masses of information to be reproduced parrot-fashion in tests and examination papers, but there was no one to help us to think about the deep issues of life. Our debating was superficial, and it was more concerned with temporal things than with matters of eternal import. Church life seemed more concerned with ritual than reality; assembly prayers at school were a mere formality; religious instruction was more like a history or geography lesson based on the Bible than teaching about God revealed as Father, Son and Holy Spirit. Indeed most of us would have identified with the young curate taking his confirmation class through the Athanasian Creed, declaring faith in 'God the Father incomprehensible, God the Son incomprehensible and God the Holy Spirit incomprehensible'. Yet amid the darkness and confusion there was still that innate sense of God being there and not yet revealed. As Søren Kierkegaard put it,

> to youth God dwells close at hand; in the midst of sorrow and joy he hears God's voice calling; if he does not hear it, then he misses it at once, if he has not learned evasion, if he does not know how to hide himself – until he hears it again. When one becomes older, then it is far to heaven; and the earthly noises make it difficult to hear the voice; if one does not hear it, then the earthly noises make it easy for one not to feel the want of it. Youth understands it at once. (S. Kierkegaard, *Edifying Discourses – A Selection*, Fontana, 1958 p. 105)

4   Several near-misses

Still hoping for the right person to help me, I kept searching during the rough and tumble of National Service life. Here I found that not everybody in the world was a neat, middle-class, suburban-type person, meandering through life with an attitude of general goodwill and utter purposelessness. Suddenly I was living amongst chaps whose spare-time hobby was to join their East London gangs wielding bicycle chains and iron bars. The culture shock for me was considerable as I found myself among the cynical, the disillusioned, and those who survived on cunning, deceit and violence. However, some real and lasting friendships were formed, but most of us who came from mild, well-mannered backgrounds were bowled over by the aggression which was constantly being released in service life. Sadly, no one at any stage spoke of living faith in Christ. No vicar or chaplain came near to help.

Unfortunately, I did come into close contact with those who were less than helpful to me in my quest. I got to know a flight sergeant who showed great interest in the young airman who was always asking for weekend passes in order to play the organ at weddings. When I was in camp over the weekend he would encourage me to stay for the service in the Station Chapel where he would be leading the worship or sometimes preaching himself. He fitted my image of an active layman, committed to regular worship and busy in church affairs. But strangely, his life at the Air Force base did not match up to his profession in chapel. He was renowned for telling dirty stories and *risqué* jokes and he curried favour with his superiors and dealt unfairly with those for whom he was responsible. This caused me to question the validity of Christianity and the church, if one of its leading proponents could live such a double life. It was not my first encounter with hypocrisy, but I fell into the trap that so many people do of judging Jesus by his disciples. I attributed inadequacy to the Lord Jesus Christ because he seemed unable to improve this person's life.

So many people make the hypocrisy of churchgoers their excuse for not going to church, instead of considering the claims of Christ upon their own hypocrisy. Jesus lived among hypocrites and had to say to some of the leading religious people of his day: 'Woe to you, scribes and Pharisees, hypocrites!' (Matt 23:13–36). His age was not peculiar or different from subsequent ages, and as he knew who was play-acting among his own contemporaries so he sorts out true from false religious practice today. Speaking to the Pharisees he said, 'God sees through you' (Luke 16:15 NEB). Just as he 'turned and looked at Peter' (Luke 22:61), piercing into the depths of Peter's personal denial of his Lord with cursing in front of a servant girl, so he looks on any unworthy discipleship as much with pity and sadness as with definite judgment. We do not need to judge the hypocrisy of others – that is God's business – but we do need to see how the church in being full of hypocrisy as well as of sincerity only proves the Bible true in its portrayal of human sinfulness and waywardness. Far from turning us away from the church, human hypocrisy should make us feel that we are at home in such company and make us cry out with others for the forgiveness and strengthening of our lives.

I could not see it that way at the time. The weakness and inconsistency of outwardly professing Christians caused me to doubt the reality of the gospel and, if anything, to keep away from the church. It was unfortunate that just as I was coming to terms with the new and tougher society in the Royal Air Force, I also encountered in a local church near the RAF base further examples of shallow Christianity. There was still no one to answer my personal queries about God and about certain statements in the Christian creeds, and I was not in the least impressed with the set-up in a local church where the vicar and organist connived so that the sermon was guaranteed to go on long enough to allow the organist and some men in his choir to pop across the road to the local pub during the sermon time. It meant that the last voluntary was merry, but it disappointed me at a crucial time of searching after God.

One person, however, impressed me. I shared a room with him for many months and he lived in a way that I could admire. He seemed to have standards for his behaviour which guided and controlled him. He never found it easy to explain to others what made him tick, but on one occasion he did pluck up the courage to invite me to a meeting in London at which Dr Billy Graham was speaking. My mind had been prejudiced against Billy Graham at that time by articles (which I subsequently found to be quite untrue) in a Sunday newspaper suggesting that he was on a money-making enterprise and was therefore not sincere in his gospel preaching. They alleged that people were planted in the huge congregations to put five pound and ten pound notes into the offertory baskets in order to encourage others to do likewise. It was only later when I met genuine Christians that I realised how untrue these accusations were, but again some of the mud that was thrown stuck, and I found myself unwilling to go to the crusade meetings with my friend because I considered the preaching to be insincere. It was several years later that I found out that my quietly spoken friend, who had no doubt prayed for me and had plucked up courage to ask me to a gospel meeting, was indeed a true believer. He was not to know that deep down inside I was searching after God, or he might have spoken more openly of Jesus Christ, but

21

looking back I am grateful for his gracious presence and for the link in the chain that he proved to be in my own pilgrimage.

These bad experiences brought me to a point of declared agnosticism. I kept going to church only to be in with my childhood friends, and I resolved most certainly to give up the practice as soon as I was free from home church influences. There was nothing in the services, apart from the music, that spoke to me. Nor was I ready to hear any definite message from the pulpit. And I guess that this was true for many in my generation. The hangover of churchgoing as a habit during wartime years persisted for a while, but then people without a living relationship with Jesus drifted away. If a vicar, curate, choirmaster or some other significant leader of their peer group left the church, they left too.

Such fickle behaviour demonstrates the shallowness of our twentieth-century understanding of what Christianity is all about. Even with the example of Jesus himself, faithful to the end, dedicated to his own followers and laying his life down in sacrifice for those who neither love him nor desire to serve him, we still have a religion of convenience. When it suits us we worship, but most of the time we choose our own thing. If we see others fail we point the finger of scorn and make it an excuse for our own lack of commitment to Christ.

Nevertheless many Christian men and women have scorned the fickle discipleship of their age and borne good testimony under immense persecution. One such was Dietrich Bonhoeffer. He was responsible for leading and teaching a generation of young men who were facing up to the pressures of the Nazi regime in Germany. Ultimately he was martyred for remaining true to Christ, and in Mary Bosanquet's biography *The Life and Death of Dietrich Bonhoeffer* (p. 196) she quotes from a letter which studied the idea of patient endurance in the New Testament. 'It is noticeable how much significance the New Testament attaches to patience,' Bonhoeffer wrote.

'"Only he who is patient receives the promises" (Matt 24:13); "only he who is patient truly bears fruit" (Luke 8:15). A faith which does not issue in patience is neither genuine nor effective . . . steadfastness is only proved through suffering . . .'

At the stage when I was prepared to give up my allegiance to the church, I did not have genuine faith. Many people who have given up the practice of church-going and have become disenchanted with their search for living faith think they have given up Christianity in forsaking what was really an outward discipline or adherence to a group of likeminded people. In fact, they have never found true Christianity at all.

5   Still searching

At this stage of fairly innocent agnosticism, I did not realise that the English word taken from the Latin equivalent of the nineteenth-century coinage 'agnostic' is 'ignoramus'. Had I known this I should not have been so bold in proclaiming my ignorance, nor should I have been so proud in professing that I did not know God. However, just as he spoke to me at key points in my life through memorable events, I found that he spoke to me even about my call to the ministry long before I knew him personally. It was again an event that stood out in my experience in a most unusual way. It happened shortly before I left home to go to the Royal Air Force, long before God was personally real in my life.

I was sitting in the kitchen at home one Saturday afternoon attempting some impossibly difficult maths homework. The only diversion near to hand was a copy of the local parish magazine. Browsing through the advertisements and reading every inconsequential detail about Brownies, Guides and Mothers' Union meetings, I came to *The Sign* inset, and my attention was riveted on an article about a group of theological students from different backgrounds who were training for the ministry. Several of them spoke of hearing a clear call from God for this task, and I was amazed at their testimony. 'How can this be?' I questioned. 'Is God as real as that?' It seemed quite impossible to me at that time, even after some ten years of regular churchgoing, that God could speak to anyone.

For me life had no rhyme or reason. I was inclined to

share the view of Voltaire that 'the end of it is dreary, the middle worthless and the commencement ridiculous'. In an educational system that taught those who endured its monotony to pass examinations, but not to think, there was little hope of finding a philosophy of existence let alone a reality of the knowledge of God.

It is not surprising that God did not have a very high rating among a generation of children brought up in war years to accept the murder of mothers and fathers and older brothers and sisters. We went to bed at night to the lullaby of the drone of German bombers, and as the wail of sirens sounded we knew that death and destruction were near at hand for many innocent people. We spent our nights shivering in the damp of hand-dug air-raid shelters that provided subterranean protection, and in daylight hours we found sport in chasing doodlebugs among the fields of Southern England. We found the churches full of old people and children, because every-one else had gone to war. Our minds were so vividly occupied with survival that God seemed distant, remote and uninterested. 'If there is a God,' I remember saying one day, 'he must be like a little Michelin X tyre-man, somewhere distant up in the sky, peeping over the top of a cloud.'

But in this parish magazine article I read about men, some of whom had returned from the war, who yet had faith in God, and who believed that he had actually spoken to them personally. 'I don't understand it,' I remember saying to myself, 'but if ever God speaks to me personally, I shouldn't be surprised if I get called to the ministry.'

Later, at RAF Padgate, the unlikelihood of finding God in the damp waste of the drab recruit centre was guaranteed. Certainly I did not find him in the cold 6.30 am queues for the nearest cold-water tap, nor did I find him in the forced heartiness of the camp chapel service. This seemed to be an exercise laid on to provide the best excuse possible to get away from any thought of worship and to get to the true conviviality of the nearest bar.

One day I visited the chapel bookstall and bought my first Bible. It had miniscule, smudged print which seemed designed to hinder anyone from arriving at the heart of its message about God revealed in Christ. There was no one at any stage to point me to the Living Word. I remember writing to Molly, then my girlfriend and now my wife, describing my search and my frustration in not finding God. The only comfort she gave me was in a sentence which – ironically – hardened the sense of God's call. 'If you go on like this,' she said, 'you will end up as a parson.' My reaction at that time was 'God forbid!' My idea of a parson was of a man unable to find a better occupation for his days, who stood up in the pulpit and read out essays about which he had no conviction, but which provided the average choir-boy with a good excuse for at least two dozen games of noughts and crosses.

The months at Padgate were crowned with no success as far as the search for God was concerned, and indeed the greatest achievement of all in those first few weeks was to obtain a cherished medical certificate with the inscription: 'This airman is not allowed to stand for any length of time – maximum five minutes', due to an ankle injury from football. Some people now maintain that the clearest evidence of God's healing activity is in the length of time I am now able to stand in the pulpit preaching a sermon!

During this time of muddled thinking about both Christianity itself and my own call in life, it was music that held me to the life of the church. I was heading for a career in music, with a place reserved for me at Oxford University. However, all my motives were wrong in studying music at Oxford. The idea stemmed back to a moment of teenage revolt against my father's words of guidance regarding a suitable career. 'What about entering the Civil Service?' he asked one day. 'Not on your life,' I replied, 'I'm not prepared to be a cog in a vast machine.' In any case, he was a civil servant and so too were both my older sisters. Simply to do the same seemed unimaginably boring. The real reason for my objection was that I was afraid of getting stuck on the very bottom rung of the ladder, and not achieving the success that my father had done. At the heart of my objection were a pride and an ambition that wanted to lead, to head something up. But with that there was an equally real lack of self-confidence, a deep fear of failure. 'What about a career in medicine then?' my father asked. 'You'll never be out of work, and doctors get paid well.' 'No, there's no chance of that,' I said. I knew my limitations – a total lack of ability in science subjects, and a tendency to faint at the sight of one small drop of blood. 'I know,' I replied, 'I'll teach music.' It was only a mini-revolt in a conversation over lunch, but the idea stuck, though my heart was not in the idea at any stage of my progress towards a musical career.

How haphazard is the life not guided by God! Without Christ there was no way I could seriously respond to the vague intimations I had been given about a call to the ministry. I was trapped, choosing a career – in order to save face with my father – for which I had neither time, inclination nor ability. The whole idea was based on negative responses, not on positive calling.

However, I was truly grateful for what music had done for me in providing confidence for public performance and building a sense of discipline through hard practice. Also in a quite remarkable way it taught me spiritual lessons. I remember with gratitude how I was bribed into proficiency in playing hymns by my father offering six-pence for every hundred hymns I played through in *Hymns Ancient and Modern*. Time and again I played through the hymnbook, little realising that it was for spiritual profit as well as for the improvement of my savings bank account.

At the time, we lived in a house which produced in me

a real childhood fear. Every night as I went up to bed it seemed to me that there was a green haze at the top of the stairs peering down with ghoulish red eyes. My task was to creep slowly up the stairs, heart pitter-pattering, and then suddenly to rush past this apparition and leap into bed. I would pull the bedclothes over my head and sing at the top of my voice 'O happy band of pilgrims' and 'Onward Christian soldiers' and then I would say the Lord's Prayer. This was a daily bedtime ritual, and little did I realise that God was already tying together the interest in music and an ability to beat the fears that the evil one produced in my life. It does not matter at all if the apparition was self-induced, or whether there was some real evil presence there – the fact remains that a small boy had vivid fears night after night and needed to cry to God for help. I never shared these fears with anyone, but the memory of this daily bedtime battle was later helpful in ministering to many other people's inner hurts and fears.

So it was that music – the calmer of childhood fears and the keeping factor which held me in to the life of the church – took me to Oxford, where God spoke to me in a life-changing way and the path of discipleship began.

6   Converted by mistake

'Come to coffee tonight then,' said Jim. On the very first day at Oxford I discovered the priorities of university life. Oxford's new and reluctant son was about to fall into the loving, grabbing clutches of members of the Christian Union who had come up early, before the start of term, to ensure that no unsuspecting but likely candidate for membership of the 'God squad' should be missed.

I was still reluctant because of my uncertainties about a musical career. I was afraid of the sheer brilliance of other musicians, and I found that I had good reason to fear the competition. Dudley Moore, for one, was among the small group of music students starting that term!

My fears had driven me to write secretly to Marks and Spencer's, enquiring about the possibility of management training with them. I did not let any of my family know about this enquiry, but I was really attracted towards such a career. It is, of course, not dissimilar in a number of ways to the work of a vicar. There is a degree of organisation, a sense of care for the staff for whom one has responsibility, and a need for belief in the quality of the goods that are offered. Fortunately some unknown staff advisor had the wisdom to tell me to take up the place at Oxford and to enquire again if I wanted to at the end of my course.

I was afraid also about my friendship with Molly. We first met in the kindergarten when she was four years old. She was a dominant child, dressed in a tartan kilt, and even at that age she was chased by a queue of male admirers. Most of them did not succeed in establishing a lasting relationship, because they could not understand her broad Scottish accent. Later we played together in the same sandpit when we were eight years old, but did not start a serious relationship until Molly was thirteen! When I went up to Oxford we had been going out together for six years and had planned our engagement. We had already bought our engagement rings, but I was nevertheless fearful that the new life at university would prove that I had not got the security or steadfastness that would enable me to be true to one girl without fail for all time. All these fears represented an immaturity that needed Christ, and it was in this state that I arrived at Keble College, Oxford and into the welcome of Christians there, who were waiting to share their faith with me.

That evening after dinner I knocked at Jim's door. I didn't know that he was a Christian and I didn't know of the elaborate scheme that was set up to help new students to faith in Christ. Imagine my surprise, therefore, when before there was even a clink of cups or a smell of coffee brewing, he suddenly rounded on me with a jagged awkwardness of manner and blurted out, 'Are you a real Christian?' My face blushed, and my spine tingled, because for several years I had been embarrassed even to mention the name of Jesus out aloud, and here I was put on the spot about matters of personal faith in a way I found almost insulting. 'Well . . . well . . . [awkward silence] . . . I suppose I am,' I said, 'I've been baptised, I've been confirmed and I always go to church.'

Nothing, you will notice, about an experience of God. No personal conversion to describe – no thrill of discovery or testimony to God's reality in my life. I could not speak, as Monica Furlong does, of an intense awareness of God's presence. She said: 'I had an experience of God so vivid and so shattering, that I knew that either God existed or I must be stark, staring mad. And I didn't feel mad, only much happier than I have ever felt in my life.' At that point in time, I was the wrong side of that sort of happening in my life. I was not looking for it and would have been frightened to talk about it.

From my response, Jim was pretty sure that I did not know Jesus yet. As we talked I kept to the externals of religion and showed no sense of excitement at having made a personal discovery of God in Jesus. There was no glad, 'Oh yes, I've known Jesus for years.' There was no talk of a gradual dawning of faith until Jesus became real, or of any dramatic turning to him like Saul on the Damascus road or C. S. Lewis on the top of a bus. I am not sure, on looking back, that Jim had got to the chapter in his handbook on personal evangelism that told him how to cope with such a reply, so with an awkward, 'Oh, I see,' he fled to the kettle with coffee-cups rattling in his hands.

In fact, I did become a Christian that term, but it was really all by mistake. There were two Christian societies in Oxford at that time with very similar initials. One was the OUCU, affectionately known as the 'Owcu', which I considered to be very respectable. It was the Oxford University Church Union, and I had received a very gracious letter inviting me to its meetings and had every intention of joining in all its activities. However, no one from the 'Owcu' ever visited me when I actually arrived, and when a student tapped at my door and introduced himself as a member of the OICCU (Oxford Inter-Collegiate Christian Union, commonly known as the 'Oycu'), I promised to go along with him to the meeting, assuming it to be the other, respectable, society. Imagine my surprise in finding Alec Motyer speaking about knowing God in a personal way through Jesus in terms which made it quite plain to me that I was not a Christian, and in a way that I had never heard anyone else speak before.

The next mistake concerned the University Sermon. Two very genteel students, whom I imagined to be members of the respectable Christian society, invited me

31

to hear the University Sermon on the first Sunday of term. I assumed that this would almost certainly be in Latin and that it was no doubt a very proper thing for a new undergraduate to attend. Little did I realise that these two were also members of the dreaded 'Oycu' and had in fact been praying for me as one of the muddled, searching new students enquiring about Christian faith. I was duly taken along to St Aldate's to hear what turned out to be a very long and thoroughly irritating sermon by Maurice Wood, who eventually became Bishop of Norwich.

The irritation was due entirely to the fact that he made frequent reference to being an Army chaplain, and this brought back memories to me of my unsatisfactory Air Force experiences. He also seemed to know me through and through. God was using him to get under my skin and to force me to admit for the very first time that I was doing no favour to God in searching after him. Indeed I was so personally unworthy in God's sight that it was only through his extreme mercy and love shown in giving Jesus to die for me on the cross that I could begin to approach him at all.

This sermon drew out all my defensive armour. After all, I was a respectable churchgoer. I had been in the choir for many years. I had indeed been baptised and confirmed. How dare this extraordinary parson challenge my fitness for the presence of God. With consummate skill Maurice used the booming chimes of Great Tom, the bell in Christchurch just over the road, ringing out in memory of those who gave their lives in the war, to emphasise the compelling knocking of Jesus at my life. The great bell rang out as he came to the climax of his sermon. 'The door to your life is closed . . . BOING . . . Jesus is knocking to come in . . . BOING . . . He's on the outside of your experience . . . BOING . . . He says to you "Behold, I stand at the door and knock" . . . BOING, BOING, BOING!'

At the end of the service I was in turmoil. I would have

run to the furthest point of Oxford to get away from the pressure, but a friend was determined to stay and listen to Maurice Wood's further explanation of steps to faith in Christ. I did not have the courage to push past him as he sat at the end of the row, so I stayed too.

At that time the words made little sense to me, but dutifully I joined the queue and took the booklet and spoke briefly to Maurice Wood as he took my name and college address. Then I was 'followed-up'. Christians came at me round every corner, from behind every pillar, and seemed to be standing on the other side of every wall. The more I ran away, the more they seemed to chase me. 'Come to the prayer meeting,' one asked. 'Come to the Bible study,' the next one suggested. And so having made a profession of faith, and with their assumption that I was a new Christian I found myself dragged into a busy round of committed Christian activity, without any personal heart-knowledge of God.

My most embarrassing moment was at the start of a mission, when the speaker failed to turn up. Tom Watson, the student in charge, suggested that we all share how God had spoken to us already that day. As one after another in the circle gave some ready word for the encouragement of others I found my colour rising and, as it came nearer to my turn, I longed for the floor to open and swallow me up. In fact, I did manage to blurt out something of what I had discovered in the beginning of my search after God, but no one knew how nearly I was lost for good.

Gradually the search became more and more sincere. I remember confusing everyone by going forward at the end of each successive Sunday night's sermon in St Aldate's. Eventually the mission – led by John Stott – started and I remember being thrilled by the power of God's word that came through his preaching. The criticism and argument and opposition had turned to a sort of internalised despair, because however I tried I just could not come through to any living reality or personal awareness of God. On the first Sunday of the mission, I professed faith again and caused further confusion among my Christian friends. Then, on the Tuesday, it happened.

After lunch I was, by mistake, reading the wrong book. I should have been reading John Stott's booklet *Becoming a Christian*, which I had been given at the mission, but instead I was reading another small pamphlet of his called *Personal Evangelism*. And suddenly everything dawned. Suddenly I could see. I could do no personal evangelism, because I did not personally know Jesus. I could help no one further than I was myself.

Abruptly, with this awareness of definitely not having an experience of Christ to share, I went into my bedroom and knelt down at my bed and took the other booklet *Becoming a Christian*, and read through it word for word. I came to the prayer at the end but wanted to pray in my own words. 'Jesus, if you are alive . . .' – and that was a big 'if', because though I had repeated many times words of affirmation about resurrection in the Apostles' Creed, the fact that he was alive was a big question mark in my mind – 'Jesus, if you *are* alive, because you have died for my sins, and I do admit that I have failed you in so many ways, please, according to your promise, come into my life. I see that you are outside my experience and I realise you have been knocking for a long time at the door of my life. I open the door. Please come in.' Suddenly the truth of what it meant for God to make a promise to me became clear. 'Thank you Jesus, you have kept your word, you have come in. Thank you Jesus.'

Immediately there was a sensation of joy and shining gladness that took me out of this world's experience. There was a sudden radiating sense of the presence of Jesus in the tiny bare-walled room. Room 4/112, Keble College, Oxford had become the gateway into heaven. I dashed upstairs to tell John Simpson, who had become my Christian friend and counsellor, that at last it had happened. At last it was real. He viewed my enthusiasm with a calm matter-of-factness that took me completely by surprise. He obviously shared my rejoicing, but it all seemed so inevitable to him and quite unsurprising. 'Right,' he said, 'we must go off and get you a decent Bible and an alarm clock.' 'What a combination!' I thought. But he explained to me on the way that a good Bible was of little use without the biggest and loudest alarm clock to get me out of bed in the morning to read it.

Shortly after that he introduced me to the 'wet flannel technique' which prevailed at the time in Keble, whereby a certain member of the Christian Union was deputed to wake the others up at half-past six with a wet flannel. This was to make sure that we had a short time of prayer together, before going back to our rooms for an extended time alone with God. How grateful I was for that shared discipline that gradually overcame my own laziness and sleepiness in the morning. How eagerly I studied the Bible, now a totally new book to me, after many years of groping through its pages in the darkness of unbelief. How exciting the shared Bible studies became and how real the answers to prayer. In the very early days of this new awareness of God's reality it was as though everything was 'me and him'. As Cardinal Newman put it, speaking of his own conversion, 'I knew two only absolutely self-evident beings, myself and my creator.' Fellowship with others, human partnership and community can be discovered later. At first though, it's me and him discovering and developing the love relationship by word and prayer.

The first genuine prayer problem concerned Molly. We had been going out together for a full six years and yet my new Christian friends made it very plain that it was not possible to contemplate a satisfactory marriage with somebody who was not a believer. Equally it was not a Christian or an honourable thing to do to jettison such a long-standing friendship so near to our engagement without doing everything possible to share my new-found faith in Jesus with her. To God there was an immediate surrender – 'Lord, here I am; I give everything up to you, even my loved one if that has to be.' To Molly there was the offer of sharing a new life, with Jesus as a new friend, with new standards, new priorities and possibly a new and revolutionised future.

Much to the dismay of Christian friends, I had a long-standing agreement to meet Molly in London on the last day of the mission. They were concerned that I should miss the climax of the mission. I was concerned that the climax of the mission for me should be that Molly might come to share my new-found faith. As we tramped the uneven pavements of London, I described every detail of my quest for truth, and my discovery of Jesus. We ended the day in Westminster Chapel listening to one in a whole series of sermons on the conversion of St Paul. 'How can she fail to see what conversion means?' I said to myself, 'The message is crystal clear.' But little did I realise that the message of Jesus, so plain to me with eyes opened to spiritual realities, was still dark and difficult to understand for Molly Anne. I went home to Oxford hopeful that night; Molly went home in the dark.

The crunch really came on the last day of term – the day of our engagement party. My Christian friends were pressing me to attend an end of term conference of Christians and to delay the engagement. 'What infernal intrusion,' I thought, and made my own mind up not to conform to their Christian behavioural pattern. Turning to God that morning, I came to the portion of Scripture set for that day. Imagine my amazement in finding that Jesus knew all about my predicament – my doubts about Molly's conversion and the rightness of giving my life to her, and the conflict presented by the demands of Christian friends. Mark 10: 7 said: 'A man shall leave his father and mother and be joined to his wife, and the two shall become one. So they are no longer two but one. What therefore God has joined together, let not man put asunder.'

All doubt was gone. God's answer was straight. Molly

was the girl for me and no one could raise any further question mark. Those rings bought four months before with some degree of hesitancy and fear about the future now became symbols of a union planned by God and prepared before the event as surely as our partnership together began and grew years before knowing Christ as our friend.

Exactly seven days later at a Billy Graham film in London, Molly was counselled and helped to faith in Christ. *Souls in Conflict* was the film – souls in concert was our experience after that.

7   If you want to grow

'Are you coming to the prayer meeting?' Every Monday and Friday evening at about ten to six my friend John Simpson would knock loudly on my door, poke his head through and make the invitation. 'Oh John, I've had such a bad day. I've been trying to get down to my essay all day long, and now I've just got going. I don't really think I can make it tonight.' I didn't let on that I had wasted hours in the early part of the day, writing letters, reading newspapers, having friends in to coffee and generally frittering the time away. C. S. Lewis wrote about it in *Screwtape Letters*, where Wormwood, a very junior devil, was given instructions in the art of tempting Christians by his uncle Screwtape.

> You no longer need a good book, which he really likes, to keep him from his prayers or his work or his sleep; a column of advertisements in yesterday's paper will do. You can make him waste his time not only in conversation he enjoys with people whom he likes, but in conversations with those he cares nothing about on subjects that bore him. You can make him do nothing at all for long periods. You can keep him up late at night, not roistering, but staring at a dead fire in a cold room. (C. S. Lewis, *Screwtape Letters*, Fount, 1977, pp. 63–64)

I knew that I had no excuse at all for not turning out to pray. I knew that in one sense it was a privilege to have been invited with praying friends into God's presence. I knew that we had seen specific answers to prayers, and that it really worked to bring people and situations to God. A number of our friends had come to a living faith in Christ despite previously having had no interest in him at all. I knew too that there were bigger issues affecting society and indeed I had discovered in Paul's first letter to Timothy that he urged that 'supplications, prayers, intercessions, and thanksgivings be made for all men, for kings and all who are in high positions, that we may lead a quiet and peaceable life, godly and respectful in every way' (1 Tim 2:1–2).

Although the discipline of daily personal prayer each morning and evening had been a hard thing to establish, none the less personal prayer was real and I was learning to talk to God not only at set times but at odd moments through the day as well. I didn't think I was very good at it, and I enormously envied a friend (now a bishop in the church) who was once psychoanalysed by a third year psychology student. He was an ex-army officer, a keen rugger player, and was greatly respected throughout college, and when he was asked what gave him more pleasure and delight than anything else in the world, he unashamedly replied: 'My times of prayer alone with the Lord.' I knew the duty, but not always the delight, and I longed to love God more and to know him better.

When I prevaricated, John just looked at me with a stern twinkle in his eye, as though I had no real excuse at all for missing forty minutes or so of prayer. My conscience was stirred and I knew just what James meant when he wrote of 'a double-minded man, unstable in all his ways' (Jas 1:8). Such a person cannot ask anything from the Lord with confidence, for the faith that would ask God for wisdom in making the right decision is replaced by doubt – 'he who doubts is like a wave of the sea that is driven and tossed by the wind' (Jas 1:6). I did not have the faith to trust God to forgive me for all the wasted time and indiscipline of the day, nor did I have faith to believe that if I put him first by going to the prayer time, that he could then strengthen me for a really useful period of concentrated work after dinner.

John could see that I was working myself up into a state of anxiety, and week after week the same tussle took place. There is something boringly repetitive about the devil's patterns of temptation, and in my heart of hearts, I knew the right thing to do every time. John's intervention at this point was always the same: 'Cast all your anxieties on him, for he cares about you.' He would remind me of the Bible reference for that verse (1 Pet 5:7) and leave me to pray it over in order to lose my anxieties and to ask the Lord what I should do. Without fail I turned up at the prayer time, rather shamefacedly, and without fail I would be signally blessed through the meeting.

I learnt through this twice-weekly battle how the enemy will do anything to keep us from prayer. P. T. Forsyth used to say: 'The worst sin is prayerlessness.' The reason is, of course, that when we fail to pray, we are saying that we do not need God's guidance and strength. The minutes taken for prayer were never wasted, because the essay which I had found so hard to complete was always finished with God's help much more quickly than if I had struggled on in my own strength.

This conflict over attending corporate prayer times was reflected in my efforts to establish a personal prayer life, both at set times morning and evening, and through each day as well. Once the brief corporate prayer time was over, there was always a lengthy time alone in our rooms before breakfast and I was helped by simple outlines of prayer topics suggested in the many handbooks on prayer that are always available from Christian bookshops. A favourite outline which appeared in almost every book I read was based on the word ACTS, the letters standing for Adoration, Confession, Thanksgiving and Supplication. I wrote these headings in a notebook and filled them out with my own topics for each day. I remember finding one pattern for prayer that always involved confessing the 'sin of worry' on Thursday morning, a sin which I would never have focused on if I had made up the list myself.

As students at Oxford, we were enormously privileged in having a room to ourselves, and I found that to have a special place with Bible, notebooks, prayer lists and books of prayers and hymns at hand was a tremendous help in establishing new habits of prayer. Sometimes I would become bored, and would go out for an early morning walk and pray out loud to God, sometimes to the consternation of a passer-by who thought I was talking to myself. Often wandering thoughts were a problem, until I learnt to pray for each person and situation to which my unruly thoughts had turned. As the devil had tried to stop me concentrating on prayer, he soon found he was beaten at his own game. The distractions of thought led to more prayer being offered, not less.

I found that so many lessons on how to pray could be learnt by reading biographies of great men of God, and by studying the lives of men of prayer in the Bible. Many have prayed in strange places. Jonah prayed from the belly of the great fish and David from the lion's den! But these were hardly the regular places for developing their devotional lives. They had learnt to turn to God when they were in danger, even though in Jonah's case he had brought the trouble on himself by running away from God's will. Jesus is supremely our example, and he never missed meeting alone with his Father in prayer: 'in the morning, a great while before day, he rose and went out to a lonely place, and there he prayed' (Mark 1:35). And it was while praying that the Holy Spirit fell on Jesus (Luke 3:21–22).

The more I established a habit of daily prayer, the harder it was to keep it up. Sometimes it was difficult to pray simply because I was over-tired. The only solution was to go to bed exceptionally early the night before, so I was often in bed by 8.30 pm in order to be up early for prayer the next morning. Because I needed rather a lot of sleep, it was the only way to succeed.

In the morning time of prayer I would cry out to God: 'Lord, keep me pure today; keep me diligent in study; keep me bold in witness; keep me true to your word.' But by the time for evening prayers, I was aware of failure at every point in my walk with God. There were impure thoughts. There was procrastination. I had failed to speak for Christ when opportunities arose, and I was troubled with a sense of total unfaithfulness to God. The words of the old Prayer Book's confession rang in my ears – 'the burden of my sins is intolerable'. I would worry over these points of failure and get up from my knees still worrying. I was often tempted to give it all up.

One day I realised that my prayer was not true prayer at all. It was little more than religious worrying in a pious posture. The real point of failure, I discovered, was in the morning prayer time. I was asking for strength but not receiving it. I cried out to God for help, but I did not claim his strength. I prayed the 'please give me prayer' but failed to claim God's promise, 'Ask, and *you will receive*, that your joy may be full' (John 16:24). Up to that point, I had been living the Christian life as though I was a dirty, ragged beggar with nothing in the bank. Suddenly I realised that spiritually I was a millionaire, and I no longer needed to live on tuppence a week. I could write out a cheque and claim my inheritance in Christ. I could live as a powerful, resourceful person as I received forgiveness for failure and strength from God for success in my Christian life.

I had, in fact, been slow in appreciating that all our praying is a response to God's promise, 'You will receive.' I had been reading my Bible diligently and found that as I spoke to God in prayer, he spoke to me through the Bible passage. I used Scripture Union notes to help me understand what I was reading, but found most help from a system of study called *Search the Scriptures* (still available from IVP) which followed a question and answer system of Bible study, with very brief explanatory notes on each passage. In answering the questions in a loose-leaf notebook, I found that as the weeks went by I was building up my own personal devotional commentary on the Bible.

It was St Augustine who once said that he had lost much time at the beginning of his Christian experience by trying to find the Lord outwardly rather than inwardly. I found this a constant battle too. It was so easy to make the Quiet Time of prayer and Bible study just an outward duty, conforming to the behaviour pattern of the group of Christians I had joined. It was possible to measure the day according to whether it had started with a 'good' Quiet Time or not. The temptation to make the inward devotion of the heart into an outward deal with God was constant, and it would have become easy to blackmail the Lord by saying: 'Lord I got up early to meet you today. I worked hard at the Scripture portion and poured out my heart in prayer. Surely that carries some reward, so that I can expect things to work out well for me over the next few hours.'

The Bible says that 'The heart is deceitful above all things, and desperately corrupt' (Jer 17:9), and it did not take me long to find out how full of pride I was, claiming the privilege of entering God's holy presence as some sort of merit in his sight. The corollary to this was to fall into the opposite trap, thinking that because of failure on my part to rise early enough for a decent time alone with God, then the day was automatically doomed. I had to learn that I was accepted by God because Jesus died for me on the cross. That I could have a good day aware of his constant companionship because, alive from the grave, he is an ever-present friend and Saviour. I had to discover victory over wrong-doing by trusting the presence and power of God's Holy Spirit in my life. At any moment of temptation I could pray an arrow prayer of help to him, wherever I was. Everything, I began to discover, hinged on the constant grace, love and mercy of God in my experience – not on whether I had had a good Quiet Time or had gone to church.

8 The Joy Way

It was a while before this truth sank in. I was confused about walking with God because I had grown up with very little knowledge of the Bible. Consequently I was ignorant of the multitudes of promises contained in the Scriptures about God's promises to keep and protect his children. As I was beginning to catch up on a misspent youth by learning verses of the Bible off by heart, I discovered that God would often highlight the lessons learnt in the morning time of Bible study by linking the teaching to some incident of the day. On one occasion I had just committed a verse from Psalm 121 to memory: 'The Lord will keep your going out and your coming in from this time forth and for evermore' (v. 8). I saw that the psalm was full of strong verbs about his strength and steadfastness in keeping, guarding, protecting and directing his people.

Later in the day, driving a borrowed car, I took a group of friends from our home church in Dorking to visit Susan, a schoolfriend of ours who was at that time attending a course in Oxford. She had been very suddenly struck down, as a teenager, with infantile paralysis but was coping marvellously with life. She went everywhere in a wheelchair and her hopes and ambitions were undimmed. On the way home from our outing with Susan, I was involved in a hair's-breadth escape from a motor accident through an involuntary action which both anticipated danger, when it was not there to be seen, and which protected us from it. At the time this was a remarkable lesson, and I could not avoid linking the

Scripture verse I had grasped hold of so firmly that morning with the incident in the car. We had all been remarkably preserved, and it was one of those occasions when all the hairs at the back of my head pricked up with fear. When the crisis was over my legs and arms were like jelly, but then I realised that though I was meant to learn the lesson of that verse in a vivid way, it was very selfish of me only to relate specific Bible promises personally to myself. God had indeed preserved us from a serious car crash, but he had not preserved Susan from paralysis.

I realised that the way God dealt with us in a world of accident, illness and death did not guarantee for the Christian a free insurance policy against trouble and difficulty. Tribulation could come to test any of us, believers and non-believers alike, in a fallen world. But even within tribulation God's promises hold true and he still intervenes in our lives to teach us the lessons of his word. George Adam Smith once said: 'It is the magic of tribulation to give innocence with experience.' Not every tribulation can do this, since some may be our own fault. If I had not been heeding God's word, looking for him 'to preserve my going out and coming in', I could have driven carelessly or drunkenly, and any tribulation following an accident would have been attributable to me. But when affliction hits us through no fault of our own, God uses the circumstance of suffering to mature and mould our lives. Susan was the supreme example to us of that happening, and as we admired her courage and perseverance we prayed that God's right word to her would keep guiding her as we had felt guarded by him on that day.

As the pattern of daily prayer and personal Bible study progressed, I began to perceive that the whole process was much more about friendship with God than about slavish duty. So many of the Bible images for the word of God coming to our lives are of something pleasing, attractive and for our own good. The psalmist says: 'I find my delight in thy commandments, which I love' (Ps

119:47). For him the sense of love, joy and delight in
God's word was rewarded: 'How sweet are thy words to
my taste, sweeter than honey to my mouth!' (v. 103). The
New Testament uses more images: Peter urges young
Christians, 'Like newborn babes, long for the pure spiritual milk, that by it you may grow up to salvation; for
you have tasted the kindness of the Lord' (1 Pet 2:2–3); it
can also be like a pruning knife (John 15:2–3) and it can be
'sharper than any two-edged sword, piercing to the
division of soul and spirit, of joints and marrow, and
discerning the thoughts and intentions of the heart' (Heb
4:12). Scripture does indeed rebuke our lives and is used
by God to cut out what is wrong in us, but it also feeds
and nourishes our spiritual lives so that we grow into the
likeness of Jesus Christ: 'All scripture is inspired by God
and profitable for teaching, for reproof, for correction,
and for training in righteousness, that the man of God
may be complete, equipped for every good work' (2 Tim
3:16–17).

I gradually learnt to see the Christian life as a relationship with God through faith in Jesus Christ, with
prayer and Bible study as key factors in the communi-
cation process. A Christian, Jesus taught, is like a branch
in the vine. That's what it means to be 'in Christ'. It is
being part of him, having his life flowing into our lives, as
surely as the sap of the vine flows through every branch.
'I am the true vine,' Jesus said, 'and my Father is the
vinedresser' (John 15:1). 'Abide in me and I in you. As the
branch cannot bear fruit by itself, unless it abides in
the vine, neither can you, unless you abide in me' (v. 4).

And having established a picture to express this inti-
mate relationship between ourselves and God, the link
between the Bible and prayer is explained: 'If you abide in
me, and my words abide in you, ask whatever you will,
and it shall be done for you' (v. 7). The governing factor in
making requests to God is that the word of Jesus abides in
our lives. Then we have his mind and we learn to pray
according to his will. Prayer ceases to be the selfish,

grasping, immature 'give me' expression of personal desires.

I pray increasingly according to the mind and will of Jesus himself, following his pattern of obedience to the Father 'unto death, even death on a cross' (Phil 2:8). As I learn to pray with this quality of submission and surrender, the problem of unanswered prayer diminishes. So many give up praying because answers do not come according to plan or expectation. Like selfish, disappointed children, some Christians sulk if the answer to their prayers is delayed, or is in the negative. So few stop to think how self-centred so much prayer is. James hit the problem on the head when he said: 'You do not have, because you do not ask. You ask and do not receive, because you ask wrongly, to spend it on your passions. Unfaithful creatures!' (James 4:2–4). It was C. S. Lewis who pointed out: 'Every war, every famine or plague, almost every death-bed, is a monument to a petition that was not granted.'

Prayer that is prayed within the mind and will of Christ himself recognises that in the agony of the garden of Gethsemane, even the heartfelt longing of Jesus that the cup of suffering might be taken away from him could not be granted. He could either run away from the suffering of our fallen world or accept it as the only way to heal and redeem the world's sorrows. Jesus did not seriously expect anything but an unanswered prayer when he asked the Father: 'My Father, if it be possible, let this cup pass from me; nevertheless, not as I will, but as thou wilt' (Matt 26:39). He knew his destiny and his commitment to the cross. He shrank from bearing the sin of the whole world on his sinless frame. And though the thought of escape clearly came into his mind, he prayed aware of his Father's ultimate good purpose: 'Again, for the second time, he went away and prayed, "My Father, if this cannot pass unless I drink it, thy will be done"' (v. 42).

The promise of Jesus regarding prayer in John 15 is not that I should have unlimited answers as I ask. It is a promise for answers to believing prayer *limited* by what is the revealed will of God in the Scriptures. But with the word of Jesus informing my life, there is an assured experience of joy: 'These things I have spoken to you, that my joy may be in you, and that your joy may be full' (John 15:11). The same experience is promised when we respond to the promises with believing prayer: 'Hitherto you have asked nothing in my name; ask, and you will receive, that your joy may be full' (John 16:24).

Canon Guy King once wrote a commentary on Paul's letter to the Philippians which he entitled *The Joy Way* (Marshall, Morgan & Scott, 1952). In the London Borough of Beckenham, where he was vicar of the parish of Christ Church, he discovered that many roads were called Ways – Bramley Way, Bushey Way, Village Way, but there was no Joy Way. In describing the Christian life, Paul speaks of joy or rejoicing over and over again, and from the promise of Jesus, too, we find that to 'walk with Him and talk with Him' brings joy as we hear and obey his word and respond through him in prayer.

The actual experience of growing in such a joyful relationship with God is so simple. Handbooks in prayer and Bible study can make it such a complicated exercise, but usually the difficulties are not about techniques or methods, but are about our obedience and surrender to God's will.

In Luke 24 we are given a picture of two disciples (possibly man and wife) walking away from Jerusalem, sad in heart following the crucifixion of Jesus. They had not stayed long enough to check out the rumours about his resurrection from the dead, and so were thoroughly disheartened as they walked to their home village of Emmaus. Then we are shown what a difference Jesus makes, even before they were fully aware that he had started walking with them. He explained the meaning of the Scriptures to them, and helped them to see the necessity of his death and resurrection. He rebuked them for being 'slow of heart to believe all that the prophets have spoken' (Luke 24:25) and finally, as he accepted their invitation to go into their home at Emmaus, they recognised him as he broke and blessed the bread and gave it to them, 'And their eyes were opened and they recognised him; and he vanished out of their sight' (v. 31). Later they told every detail of their meeting with the risen Jesus to the other disciples, and he appeared to them all again to confirm the reality of their experience. When Jesus finally left them 'and was carried up into heaven . . . they returned to Jerusalem with great joy, and were continually in the temple blessing God' (vv. 51–53).

This Joy Way of friendship with God through Jesus Christ is confirmed in an old story about a man called Jim, who had a very simple faith. He was not a man of books and had little learning at all. But each lunch time he left his work in the fields to go into the quietness of the nearby village church. He knelt in silence and then prayed – just three words: 'Jesus, it's Jim.' This went on throughout his working life. Then he became ill and could not keep up his habit of simple devotion. Lying near death on his bed one day, Jim had a startling and marvellous experience. It was as though a shining figure came to the end of his bed, and in the quietness he too spoke just three words: 'Jim, it's Jesus.'

I was beginning to discover this intimacy of relationship with Jesus in prayer, but there were still areas of self-discovery, and above all guidance concerning my future calling in life, that were very murky indeed. Self-discovery during those first days of knowing that God really existed was painful in the extreme. It was amazing to realise that hardly any action was proposed or any project planned without my own interest and concern being at the centre of everything. I looked back over my friendships and realised that with the sole exception of my friendship with Molly Anne, every one had been initiated from others to myself. Indeed, I was so fundamentally shy that it dawned on me that at college I really only spoke to those who spoke to me and I only became friends with those who befriended me. But Jesus had not been shy with me, he had loved me, and certainly if he had not first loved me I would never have got to know him. Suddenly I realised that this was true with other people too. He loved them and wanted me to reach out to them just as Christians had brought his friendship to me. I began to see that other people without Jesus were as afraid of me as I had been of them when I was without him, and suddenly Jesus and I together became a tremendous majority.

It was this fundamental release from fear that made it possible to think about God's call to the ministry. Reading the Bible made it plain that God was good at taking people who felt basically unworthy of serving him and using them for a marvellous purpose. 'I am not worthy', 'I am not eloquent', 'I am a young man', 'I am unclean' – all these were excuses used by people just discovering the reality of God, to keep them from serving him. All these were excuses in my thinking.

But I had a problem. It was music that had held me so much to the life of the church. Church music had been the means of discovering the little I had known about God before this recent cataclysmic encounter with Christ. Within a purist musical tradition, there was no room for the sort of gospel hymns which my Christian friends sang so heartily; there was no room for the pietistic sentiments and paltry harmonies of so much that was a vehicle of regular worship in the circles I had entered. My tummy squirmed at some of the choruses we sang, and I felt a conflict that affected my integrity as a musician.

But God has a way of dealing with the paradox of our feelings of unworthiness and our pride. I was taken one Sunday to a remarkable church in Reading by two friends, Stewart Symons and John Simpson. Stewart had been helped there during his time in the Royal Air Force and was determined that we should share the benefits of its ministry. The service was packed and the impact of a full congregation made a tremendous impression on me as a new young Christian. Doubtless few of the Christians who attended that night will remember that particular service, and yet the obedience of their worship was used by God to call out three men to three lifetimes of daily ministry in the Church of England. The preaching of John Page, the vicar, was an unleashing of verbal thunderbolts. The singing was hearty but, to a proud musician in training, left much to be desired. However, one thing was certain – God was there!

After the service we went to the adjoining hall for tea, biscuits and 'fellowship'. Apparently this was a very typical and traditional happening in that sort of church. Soon we settled down in rows and one after another chose a hymn and gave their reasons for choosing it. 'Help and horrors' was my initial reaction. 'All these ghastly evangelical hymns!' But then in the course of the hymn singing each of my friends in turn spoke of how God seemed to be calling them to the ministry and I was aware of being put on the spot myself. 'If I were to respond to a call to the ministry, how could I help in bereavement situations and meet people in the sadness of life?' 'Furthermore', I thought, 'how can I endure these terrible hymns?'

My heart sank as a lady then chose 'Blessed assurance, Jesus is mine' – my particular pet hate at the time. But when the vicar asked why she chose it she gave her reason. 'It's because this hymn is what God used to comfort me and my family during this week when my little grandchild was knocked down and killed by a car.' I froze inside and the meeting hushed in praying sympathy with that family in its bereavement. And suddenly everything was clear to me – God could take what I despised to minister in a situation where I had no resources to help. Suddenly I saw what ministry was about: it had a divine source, it represented a divine working in human lives.

I gave no testimony that night but remember travelling

home on the train trying to get on my own in the corridor. 'Are you really speaking to me Lord? Is this just a ghastly pride? Is the insecurity of my future now settled? What about Molly? And my parents? But Lord, I have never preached in my life. And how could I live without being on the organ stool and training a choir?'

The questions were unresolved when I got back to my room at midnight, but in prayer my musical tradition again came to my rescue. I recalled an anthem which I had so often sung in the past in my home church in Dorking. The words came from Psalm 5 and the music was by S. S. Wesley:

> Lead me Lord, lead me in Thy righteousness
> Make Thy way plain before my face.
> For it is Thou Lord, Thou Lord only
> That makest me dwell in safety.

And I knew that was it. At last the mystery of my calling in life was clear, and though there were many hesitancies and many practical difficulties to overcome, for the first time in my life the way ahead seemed a Joy Way indeed.

9   That Monday morning feeling

The problem was Monday morning. Jack, the college
scout, called with his usual cheery 'Good morning' and
poured steaming hot water from his enamel jug into the
old-fashioned washing bowl. Although it was January
1955, Keble College had not quite moved into the twen-
tieth century as far as running hot and cold was concerned. I washed and shaved, quickly dirtying the
meagre supply of water. The soapy pool seemed to
represent the poverty of what I had to offer God. I
remembered that Jesus spoke of rivers of living water
flowing through our being to refresh a thirsty world, but
overwhelmed with a classic Monday morning feeling,
doubts came thick and fast. Was that really a call to
the ministry? Was that how God speaks? Would that
midnight prayer change my whole life? And what
about Molly Anne? These and other jumbled thoughts
brought question marks to the emotionalism of the night
before.

If the decision was merely emotional it would surely
not stand examination by Monday's questions. Already
Monday mornings had become established as the devil's
best time to sow questionings and doubts about the
reality of my Christian experience and the genuineness of
my faith. I did not recognise the tactics for several weeks,
but eventually the 'coincidence' of the Monday pattern
had to be noticed. It was as obvious as the temptation of
Jesus in the wilderness following his baptism experience
and the failure of the disciples after seeing the glory of
Jesus on the Mount of Transfiguration. Every weekend at

Oxford was a time of special learning and of deep Christian fellowship. Indeed, the normal Sunday programme demanded the strength and stamina of a mountaineer in order to survive. The morning started early with Holy Communion in the College Chapel and after breakfast there was an exodus from all the colleges in Oxford in order that Christian Union members might join together in a central united prayer time before going on to various local churches. After lunch a small group, mostly of those considering a call to the ministry, met for another time of prayer in College and later in the afternoon we set off on cycles to visit patients and lead services in various local hospitals. With a downhill run back to College there was just time for Evening Chapel, and after a meal in Hall there would be yet another service, this time in the city centre, to which we would take our friends. With every Sunday providing such a spiritual assault-course, it was not surprising that Monday blues overtook the young Christians.

For me the temptation was quite simple. After Monday breakfast I would itch and scratch over some difficult piece of academic work, knowing that it must be finished quickly because of a deadline later that day. But inspiration never came. After a fruitless and frustrating hour I would throw in the sponge and decide to look around the bookshops in town. Cycling even through rain and storm, I would feel like some modern-day Jonah pulled relentlessly away from the course of duty to a self-chosen task. It seemed reasonable enough. What harm could there be in looking around the second-hand bookshops? It even seemed a godly thing to browse in the theological departments! But that was where the trouble began. Week after week, I would take down some dusty, musty volume which some sensible person had discarded years before, and I would turn the pages inconsequentially. I would come across a passage which plainly and specifically contradicted the positive truth which I had learnt that very weekend from the Bible. After this happened several times, the coincidence of it was beyond belief. The Christian Union Committee had invited the speaker perhaps more than a year before. His theme had been chosen by a committee several months before. The speaker had prepared his talk many miles away, perhaps little realising the power and impact it would have on young Christians in his audience. And then at the end of such a complex process the truth that had been so gladly received on Saturday or Sunday was snatched away each Monday morning.

It was a confused and unbelieving undergraduate who pedalled his way disconsolately back to College after this unequal jousting with the theological giants of former days. Any memory of mountain-top glory had gone completely, and Monday morning failure was complete. But when the pattern of temptation became clear it was possible to counter it. The answer was found in learning a moment by moment dependence on God. 'Lord,' I would cry, 'please help me concentrate for the next ten minutes. Please help me produce some written work. Please help me to work well now.' And then only ten minutes later, with more work done in that ten minute period than I had previously been able to complete in two hours, I would realise that God had answered my prayer. It does not always work out that a Christian gets quick and glib answers to prayer, but at this stage of spiritual immaturity the prayers and the answers were meaningful.

In the cold light of day, it was no easy thing to be clear about such a revolutionary happening as my apparent call to the ministry. But decisions had to be made. A letter to Molly Anne, a letter to my parents, and then second thoughts about the subject I was reading. Music had seemed the obvious choice to study at Oxford, but now the call to the ministry highlighted a nagging doubt. For several weeks I had experienced increasing difficulty in hearing properly. This had never been a problem before, but it was now so pronounced that I could not distinguish notes even a fifth apart, and now a psychological panic had made it impossible to do the simplest ear-tests. Only when I changed to a degree course in English did my hearing return to normal. It seemed a safe way of guidance at the time, and a mark of God's overruling, in that it was possible to change so easily and that professors and parents combined to agree in their advice.

But another difficulty seemed even more daunting. Molly and I were already engaged to be married, and had been friends for more than six years. Soon the facts emerged concerning ordination. The diocese advised waiting for some years after ordination rather than taking on holy orders and a wife at one and the same time! The only alternative was to get married some years ahead of ordination, and this seemed quite impossible to contemplate because we could not afford it.

If we followed the bishop's advice and planned to delay marriage until several years after ordination, both of us had to be willing for a very long wait. Four years at Oxford, followed by two years at a theological college, plus more years waiting to get married after ordination, presented a daunting prospect. I did not know how to break the news to Molly. 'Do you realise that if I was to be ordained, we might have to wait another nine years before we could get married?' I deliberately painted it as black as I could, though there was some hope that it might have been a year or two less than that.'Would you be willing to wait for me?' I asked. After only a moment's pause the answer came. 'Of course I will,' Molly replied, 'If God has called you, then we're in it together.'

We had to live with that decision for two years, but as the time for ordination drew nearer we had to make firm plans for the future. I was to be ordained by the Bishop of Guildford, whose rules caused the problem in the first place. He strongly suggested that we should marry sooner rather than later. The Warden of Keble College and the Principal of Oak Hill College agreed. Oak Hill was the Anglican theological college in London which I was due to attend after completing my degree course at Oxford, and it was important that the Principal agreed to our marriage. Molly and I then had to appear before the whole of the Surrey County Council Education committee to see if they would continue to support us financially. At the time of our interview Molly was working in a large mental hospital, teaching dressmaking skills to many of the patients. Her pay was modest, but because of her wage my grant was drastically reduced. It was a very testing time, and neither of us found it easy to deal with such senior, imposing men investigating our circumstances. However, when it was all sorted out, Molly and I married on exactly the same Saturday that we would have chosen if we had said, 'No, Lord, we will not serve you this way. The cost is too great.' When the wedding bells rang on the first Saturday after my last day of term at Oxford, my mind went back to those times alone with God in room 4/112 Keble College Oxford, as the chimes and bells from many a dreaming spire combined with the thud and clunk of Keble's own clock, to ring in each new day.

10   Witness to the truth

'If you're home later than half-past nine, you're never going to one of those Bible meetings again.' That was the exaggerated reaction of Molly's mother soon after we both came to know Christ, and had begun to find our voracious appetite for the word of God satisfied through the regular Bible teaching sessions of the Abinger Convention. Such meetings were a lifeline to those who had to live in an area where the mainstream churches were not renowned for excelling in a Bible teaching ministry. The main convention was held every summer in a large marquee in the village of Abinger, half-way between Dorking and Guildford. Hundreds of Christian people gathered every day to enjoy a week of Bible teaching given by the leading preachers of the day. Every month throughout the year a rally was held in the village hall which followed the same pattern as the main convention meetings.

The sharp reaction of Molly's mother illustrated the sort of conflict that young Christians often meet in family life. She was not deeply opposed to things Christian, indeed she was a regular churchgoer who responded as well as she could within the cool Anglicanism of our home church. However, in those days people were rather traditionally divided into their Church of England or Nonconformist slots, and much of our trouble at home started because of the local Baptist minister's faithful follow-up to Molly's stand for Christ at a Billy Graham film. 'We're Church of England and always have been' was the response of Molly's mother, as she envisaged the

59

scandal of her daughter linking up with the local Baptists.
She need not have worried; much as we came to respect the Christian people at the local evangelical
Baptist church, it was always clear to us that our call
was to be as faithful and regular as we could be within the context of the church in which we had grown
up.

I am sure that at times our zealous witness caused
distress to the vicar and to those with whom we worshipped, but the clergy encouraged us in starting Bible
study and prayer groups for young people. Even if they
disagreed with our badly expressed and ill-formed theology, they were kind enough to be so tolerant that we
were never pushed out of the church in which we grew
up. Indeed, as the years have gone by, we look back with
increasing thankfulness for the church that cradled our
new life in Christ.

One of the clergy 'encouraged' me with the words:
'Don't worry Tom, you'll soon grow out of it,' as I shared
my testimony of the living faith in Jesus Christ that I had
discovered at university. However, he was not at all
off-putting in the long run. He was simply expressing the
hope that I would grow up, rather than remain with an
immature and infantile experience of Christ. At the time I
was inclined to be judgmental and critical of his advice,
because he seemed to be saying that a conversion experience is something transitory and emotional and is of very
little value in the ongoing Christian life. In one sense that
is true, because unless I am going on in the Christian life,
and repenting and believing in Christ every moment of
every day, then my initial profession of faith might have
been a matter of 'believing in vain' (cf. 1 Cor 15:2). James
says that faith needs to be 'completed by works' (Jas 2:22),
and in a dramatic phrase he says that: 'a man is justified
by works and not by faith alone' (Jas 2:24). I needed at
that stage to be reminded that a dramatic declaration of
faith and a fervent testimony is not the guarantee of
God's working in our lives. If his Spirit is in us, he will

produce fruit in a new Christlikeness of character and in
persevering obedience to the will of God.

It was one thing to argue about matters of faith and
doctrine with the clergy and other friends in the local
church. It was quite another thing to be consistently
Christlike at home where parents and relatives knew our
failings only too well. For example, was it right to stop
going to Christian meetings that got us home after 9.30
pm? Where did 'Honour your father and your mother'
(Exod 20:12) come into this? The natural man argued that
for years we had been accustomed to staying out until the
early hours of the morning for a friend's birthday party or
some other special celebration. Why should we obey
such an unreasonable demand? After all, we were both
over twenty-one and engaged to be married. After
praying about it, Molly and I soon came to the conclusion
that the only telling witness that we could make was to
humble ourselves and contain our own angry reaction to
such a ridiculous rule and in fact to do everything in our
power to submit to the parental request. It meant that we
had to face many early nights during our courting days,
but it led to harmonious family relationships, and ultimately Molly's mother came to clear Christian faith before she died. It is the scriptural way to obey parents, and
our action proved the Bible true when it says 'Good sense
makes a man slow to anger' (Prov 19:11). I was also
reminded of one of my own mother's favourite sayings:
'A soft answer turns away wrath' (Prov 15:1).

A young Christian can find other pitfalls in working
out his Christian obedience in the context of nominally
Christian family life. There was one occasion when Molly
and I were due to drive my parents to Scotland for a
holiday. We were towing a caravan, and they felt that at
all costs they had to spend Sunday completing the long
journey and then for their own health's sake to remain
settled and still for some days at a Scottish caravan site.
Molly and I were strongly sabbatarian at the time and
objected strongly to driving on that one day in seven

61

when we wanted to be still and worship God in a nearby church. We had not yet worked out the difference between the Old Testament sabbath and the Lord's day. It seemed as though we were torn apart between two equally valid commandments – 'Honour your father and your mother' (Exod 20:12) and 'Remember the sabbath day, to keep it holy' (Exod 20:8). In the end we chose to drive on the Sunday because we felt that my parents would never understand our scruples, and though Paul seems to qualify the command, 'Children, obey your parents *in the Lord*' (Eph 6:1), we felt that our Christian witness would tell most strongly to our parents if we conformed to their wishes. God's bonus to Molly and myself, and somehow his confirmation of the rightness of our decision, was that at the end of the journeying on that Sunday we found a small church with its door still open, and long after the normal service time we were able to be together in a quite memorable act of worship, just on our own with the Lord.

Another point of conflict came over our wedding. Molly and I were going through a very black and white phase as far as the use of alcohol was concerned, and it was our wish that we should have no alcohol at all at our wedding reception. However, when my parents heard of this they were appalled. Neither set of parents could understand our scruples: they felt that if modest drinks were not provided they would appear inhospitable to all the members of the family who came to celebrate the wedding. They felt that we were insulting both families by suggesting that alcohol would be unwisely used, and, as trivial issues have a habit of doing at the time of making wedding plans, this matter got totally out of proportion. We recognised our fault in not appreciating the hurt we were causing and the offence we were giving, and in the end surrendered our point of view. I am sure that in the long run that particular compromise had a better effect in terms of Christian witness than if we had stuck to a legalistic principle.

These may seem very small concerns, but they illustrate the controversy that Satan loves to stir within family
life when young Christians seek to witness to their faith
at home. It can often be part of Satan's strategy to get us
into a situation where in attempting to give verbal witness to the love of Jesus we end up in bitter argument
over quite secondary matters of Bible doctrine. The
Christian argues vehemently for what is no more than a
point of view, or a matter of interpretation, as though the
whole validity of Christianity stands or falls on whether
or not the argument is won. I found this often happened
in matters of churchmanship, where so often the genuine
desire to witness to someone of another persuasion led to
bitter and disparaging words. The devil loves to do the
same today, and he has a clever way of destroying
friendships by setting up equally sincere Christians within different groupings against each other so that in their
desire to 'witness to the truth', they split up and divide
among themselves instead of uniting to witness to the
world.

Satan's trick is to get Christians to seize on one point of
Bible teaching which is particularly representative of
their group or church and judge all other Christians in the
light of that one point of doctrine. For example, after Billy
Graham's greatly used preaching at the Villa Park stage
of Mission England in July 1984, there were letters in the
Birmingham press that claimed that he did not preach the
gospel, because he called people to come to Christ with
repentance and faith, but did not emphasise that they
must 'believe and be baptised'. I personally heard him
preach a whole range of Bible theology from creation to
issues of judgment and the future state beyond this life,
in a tradition of Christian exegesis that goes right back
beyond the classic creeds to apostolic teaching itself. But
he was written off and undermined publicly by some
because he did not express the call to commitment in the
words they would choose.

'Baptist' Christians have been known to hound those

who have not been baptised their way and to insist on rebaptism for those who have been baptised as the infants of believing parents. 'Anglican' Christians have been known in pride to consider their church the only one to get things right in a truly biblically balanced way. 'Housechurch' Christians seem to write off all other mainstream denominations; and when they are put on the defensive, those of other denominations can be vastly critical of the housechurch movement. 'Navigator' Christians or 'Campus Crusade' Christians can seem to be in rivalry with 'Christian Union' Christians, and instead of all working together for the kingdom cause, these different groups can so easily seem to be at variance with one another.

The game Satan gets Christians to play is a very obvious one. Each group of Christians comes to value the strengths of the movement or of the church party to which it belongs. The particular strength is then held up as the ideal norm to which all other Christians should conform. Christian witness or testimony then becomes associated with a particular doctrinal stance or a form of organisation or pastoral care.

One of our church members felt called to overseas service, and found the brochure for a college of American origin, now based in England, which offered to train missionaries for Bible translation work among unevangelised tribes. The prospectus demanded response to a particularly narrow basis of faith, and I warned our candidate that she might find herself uncomfortable with the style of Christianity expressed at the college. And so she did. Their idea of witness was to testify to their particular views on the inspiration of Scripture and to their doctrines about the last things. If a Christian could not subscribe to their view of things, exactly their way, then he or she was definitely 'out'. Instead of being accepted as a sister in Christ and as a fellow missionary willing to give her whole life in God's service, our embryo missionary found herself treated more like a child of the devil because she did not cross every 't' and dot every 'i' of their particular basis of faith. Furthermore, they were suspicious of her because of the church background from which she came. The witness of that college was to a set of interpretations of truths – not to the truth as it is in Christ himself.

Jesus said: 'You shall be *my* witnesses' (Acts 1:8). The power of the Holy Spirit is given to his disciples in order to bring glory to Jesus. Speaking of the Holy Spirit, Jesus said: 'He will glorify me, for he will take what is mine and declare it to you' (John 16:14); 'he will bear witness to me; and you also are witnesses, because you have been with me from the beginning' (John 15:26–27). At the start of his first letter, John again emphasises that Christian testimony is first and foremost testimony to Jesus himself: 'That which was from the beginning, which we have heard, which we have seen with our eyes, which we have looked upon and touched with our hands, concerning the word of life – the life was made manifest, and we saw it, and testify to it' (1 John 1:1–2).

Indeed, far from Christians dividing among themselves because of different doctrinal emphases, their agreement in unity in Christian witness to Jesus is meant to convince the world that he was sent as Saviour by the Father. Jesus prayed for this oneness to be the characteristic experience of true believers:

I do not pray for these only, but also for those who believe in me through their word, that they may all be one; even as thou, Father, art in me, and I in thee, that they also may be in us, so that the world may believe that thou hast sent me. (John 17:20–21)

His desire was that 'they may become perfectly one, so that the world may know that thou hast sent me and hast loved them even as thou hast loved me' (John 17:23).

What we have 'seen and heard' of Jesus is our valid possession, and we have the right and the duty to share it with others. Some Christians seem dissatisfied with a testimony to a living relationship with Jesus and to having the privilege of knowing him in a personal way. They seem to need a daily or weekly miracle to which they can testify, and will regale their friends with stories of remarkable guidance and dramatic happenings to enhance their reputation as devoted Christians.

In *Renew us by your Spirit* I have myself told of certain instances of remarkable guidance and special provision, but normally a Christian is slow to draw attention to himself as the recipient of special favours from God. Usually, as with Mary, we do well to dwell upon God's marvellous working in our lives in a private and personal way. This happened after the angels had revealed the coming of Jesus as Messiah to the shepherds. They found their way to the place where the Holy Family was staying, and reported what they had been told to Mary. Everyone 'wondered at what the shepherds told them. But Mary kept all these things, pondering them in her heart' (Luke 2:18–19).

Of course, by holding testimony meetings at which we encourage people to share what God is doing for them – in order to stimulate the faith of others in the Christian fellowship – we put pressure on Christian humility. A balance has to be struck in the giving of testimonies, and our motives need to be examined. I often find that the truly humble person comes after the meeting to say that they should have shared something, but did not have the courage to do so. Having missed their opportunity, the mood of the meeting changed, and they never had another chance to contribute what they should have done. I always counter the feeling of failure and remorse, and even of disobedience to God's prompting, by encouraging the person to share their testimony at the next possible opportunity, and I make a mental note to make it easy for them to do so. When such a testimony is shared at cost to the individual concerned, there is always a tremendous sense of God-givenness, and the glad response of other Christians to the word that is spoken is in sharp contrast to the disillusionment that follows self-centred and sometimes fabricated testimony.

Christian testimony to outsiders is no different. Sometimes when witness is given at an evangelistic meeting, there is such exaggeration both of the extent of sinfulness before conversion and the joy and peace and blessing of the post-conversion experience, that the testimony hardly rings true to the outsider. In all our relationships we are called to 'speak the truth in love' (Eph 4:15), and it is no help to anyone to exaggerate both the sinfulness of sin and the bliss of the new life. Of course in Bible terms, as we measure ourselves against God's goodness, it is impossible to exaggerate either of those things, but in human experience, it is easy to dress up the facts so that our life story becomes nothing more than fiction. It was Oliver Cromwell who insisted on being painted 'warts and all', and the task of any Christian testimony is to give the most truthful presentation of our real experience in Christ that we possibly can.

In person to person contact, because we are concerned only to communicate the truth, it is vital that the truth of Jesus is conveyed not only in the word of Christian testimony but in the witness of Christian life as well. We have all been troubled by the loud-mouthed, boorish Christian who insists on thrusting his experience down our throats. The very attitude that allows such a trampling upon the privacy and sacredness of other people's personalities betrays the self-centredness of the attempt to express Christian witness. Such behaviour is sometimes justified by those who do it from the final commission of Jesus himself: 'Go therefore and make disciples of all nations' (Matt 28:19). But in the earlier mission of the seventy disciples, when Jesus 'sent them on ahead of him, two by two, into every town and place where he himself was about to come' (Luke 10:1), it was evident that by their behaviour the disciples were intended to prepare the way for Jesus and to make it easier for him to come into the lives of the people in the town he was about to visit. Aggressive, self-projecting witness makes it more difficult for Jesus to enter a person's life. He asked for attitudes of perfect courtesy – 'Whatever house you enter, first say, "Peace be to this house!"' (Luke 10:5). He urged his disciples to sustain normal human relationships – 'And remain in the same house, eating and drinking what they provide . . . Whenever you enter a town and they receive you, eat what is set before you' (Luke 10:7–8).

In practice this can be quite costly at times. As a young curate in my first parish I visited an old lady who was over ninety years old. To celebrate the occasion she insisted on getting her best china down (with my help) from the very top row of hooks of a Welsh dresser. The cups looked as though they had not been washed for at least fifty years. Inside they were thick, really thick, with solid grime which seemed to crawl around the cup as you looked at it. She went outside to make the tea, and because she was herself half-blind, she then poured it into the cups without a hint of washing or wiping the filthy grease away. With a smile of triumph, so pleased to be exercising hospitality again, she passed me the murky liquid. I remembered the scripture 'eating and drinking what they provide' (v.7), so I drank, at the same time praying a silent prayer of protection.

The call to us in our witness is to be 'whole' people, whether in our family life, our church life, or in our relationships with non-Christians. So many who are enthusiastic in talking for Jesus do not live consistent and Christlike lives. Those who shoot verbal bullets most powerfully often hinder others coming to faith in Christ if their lives are not courteous, careful and Christlike. In Colossians 4:5–6 Paul says: 'Conduct yourselves wisely toward outsiders, making the most of the time. Let your speech always be gracious, seasoned with salt, so that you may know how you ought to answer everyone.' This recommendation comes after teaching about all relationships of life – in the church (Col 3:12–17); in the home, with particular reference to wives, husbands, fathers and children (Col 3:18–21); and at work, asking workers to be obedient and masters to be just and fair (Col 3:22–4:1). Then, in relation to the world, Paul asks us to be watchful in prayer, bold in speaking God's word, and wise in our behaviour and witness (Col 4:2–6).

Christian witness is part of a total life experience, and just as Jesus was fully human and fully divine, so we need to have real humanity in our relationships as the divine Spirit lives in our hearts. Paul urges us to be careful in the initiative we take in witnessing to others. We need to win a hearing by the consistency of our Christian living, and even then we do well to give an answer to questions that people are actually asking, rather than jumping in with all guns firing Bible texts at our victim.

I had a vivid experience of this when I first started doing a milk round while on my long summer vacation from university. My childhood experiences on my uncle's dairy farm were an excellent preparation for this job. The hardened milkman who took me around on the first few days was not so sure of this. He could not imagine that an embryo theological student could do a man's job! I could sense that he was eyeing me up and down very carefully during the time that we worked together, finding out whether I could drive the electric milk float properly and whether I could keep the books accurately. All the time we were establishing a friendship, I was praying that God would give me an opportunity to speak for Christ. 'Please Lord, make him ask me a question,' I prayed. 'Please open his mouth!' The exclamation marks in my prayer got more and more frequent as we came to the very last day together, and to the last journey back to base before I was due to do the milk round on my own. 'Lord, is he going to speak to me, or will I have to barge in and speak directly to him about Jesus?,' I asked.

Suddenly he turned to me as we were slowly climbing

the last hill before we arrived at the depot, and he said:
'What does it mean to get converted?' I nearly fell out of
the van through the open doorway. 'What does he mean
by that?,' I thought. I could not tell at that moment
whether he meant religious conversion or not. I guessed
that he might have assumed that because I was going to
get ordained, that this was in fact the case. So I asked him
what he meant. 'Oh,' he replied, 'it's just that a neigh-
bour of mine who used to be a milkman working for the
same firm got converted a few months ago. His life is so
different now that I just wondered what it was all about.'

I was immediately able to illustrate the difference
Christ had made to this man's life in terms my friend
could understand. One of the vans back at the depot had
recently been converted by having its clapped out petrol
engine replaced by a new diesel engine. 'It's like having a
new power source in our lives. When Jesus comes into
our hearts by his Holy Spirit it's just like the Ford van
with its new engine. To be converted is to turn from our
sin and to trust Jesus, who gives us forgiveness through
his death on the cross and power through his resurrection, and new ability to go God's way through his Holy
Spirit.'

In fact our conversation led me into new pangs of
conscience. One of the difficulties I had faced in taking on
this vacation job was that I had to work on Sundays,
when I should have preferred to be at worship. 'Is it right
for a Christian to work on the Lord's day?,' I asked
myself. I then realised that this was a stupid question,
since many Christians obviously had to work in main-
taining essential services in the community. I then
argued that it was not really necessary to do some jobs. A
milkman, for example, need not deliver milk on a Sunday, since people could have a double order on Saturday.
But then I saw that in any case, many people in the milk
industry would still have to do Sunday work, since cows
had to be milked, and the churns had to be collected from
the farm gate, before the milk went sour. I realised that

legalistic sabbatarian arguments did not really work, because even if I took up an individual stand on this issue, and refused either to have milk delivered on a Sunday, or refused to deliver it myself, there was no way I could make it possible for everyone to avoid work on the Lord's day.

The reason for all these questionings was that the milkman who had recently been converted had given up his job in order to be free to worship God regularly, and to belong to his local church. This challenged my own decision to do a vacation job that clashed with Sunday worship, and I had to determine whether this was truly God's call for me, or whether I had made a mistake that would hinder my Christian walk.

The first day I did the round on my own was awful. Molly, by that time my fiancée, gave a hand. All over the town young children were heard to cry out to their mothers: 'Mummy, that's my Sunday school teacher,' or elderly ladies called out to their companions: 'It's little Tommy who plays the organ at church.' In those days it was considered somewhat indignified to serve the community by delivering their daily pinta!

But the worst thing of all was that long after the morning service at church had finished, and several hours later than all the other roundsmen, I dragged back to the milk depot, with the van almost at the end of its battery charge, feeling a total failure. I wondered if I had made a mistake in taking on a 'man's' job, and I think the dairymen wondered if they had made a mistake too. However, within a few days speed and stamina were both achieved, and eventually it was possible to start before dawn on a Sunday morning and finish the whole round before morning service time.

The comfort of being able to sing Christian choruses, hymns and spiritual songs was considerable as I journeyed from house to house, often in appalling weather conditions. The sense of fruitfulness in witness calmed my fears about transgressing sabbath law. I soon came to realise that some essential services have to be carried out on other people's day of rest, and that there is a world of difference between a legalistic approach to sabbath observance, and the joy of being free and able to worship God on the Lord's day, the day of resurrection celebration. Up to that point I had fallen into the Puritan trap, which G. K. Chesterton said is 'to pour righteous indignation into the wrong things'.

11   An angel intervenes

Grandad Porter was a tough nut to crack. He was a Victorian by birth and style of life, and would regale his grandchildren with stories of how in the early years of the century he would drive a primitive bone-shaking motor car with old-fashioned lamps giving uncertain light on the darkened road. He was in fact Molly's maternal grandfather and represented a strong and dominating influence in her childhood years. For me too, having no childhood recollections of my own grandfathers, he represented a significant patriarchal figure in the family background. So much so that it seemed hard, almost impossible, to communicate our Christian faith with him when we first met Christ. In fact it seemed that he had been considerably put off the church in our own home town because of some misdemeanour of a curate at the parish church which he was never quite able to forgive – a warning that our actions can bring people nearer to Christ or can hinder them for years.

Grandad was the arch-disciplinarian, but in his work as a foreman gasfitter was very much respected by other men, and at every stage of his life he was a man's man. The reputation that the church has in some parts of being a club for women did not help his manliness to surrender to Jesus the Lord. His negative experiences blocked all possibility of a re-think, and it seemed to us that he had a completely closed mind to all matters concerning the Christian faith.

The shattering day came when this man who had been so fit and strong all his life suddenly fell seriously ill.

Because he had represented such a security factor in our experience, and had given the impression of being able to go on and on forever, we were taken completely by surprise and found ourselves strangely ill-equipped to cope with the sudden serious illness of such a loved member of our family. It is amazing how we are trained and educated for health, but given very little preparation for coping with our own illness or that of others. He was quickly admitted to hospital, and it was discovered that he had cancer. There was talk at first of amputating his arm, but mercifully he was spared this ordeal.

By this time we were training for the ministry in London, and it was not easy to visit him in hospital in Guildford on a regular basis. Whenever we did so, we ended up blaming ourselves for not being more bold in sharing Christ, now that he had become a captive audience in a hospital bed. Still he seemed gruff and ill-disposed to open up on any matter of personal faith. With no previous experience of illness and incapacity he responded badly to hospital conditions and was, to say the least, a cantankerous and difficult patient. He seemed almost to prefer those who would speak about worldly matters and who would try to jolly him along with superficial conversation and tritely hopeful talk. We saw him as being desperately in need of knowing Christ, and we longed that we should be able to help him to find the Christian way.

One Monday evening we visited Grandad Porter again. It was a discovery of transfiguration. Here was the wizened figure of a man smiling brightly, with a glint in his eyes and a finger beckoning us closer towards him. 'You'll never guess what's happened,' he said. 'A minister came into the ward yesterday morning and took a ward service. He was miles away at the end of the ward and I could not see him at all, and could hardly hear him. But then a figure in white came to the end of my bed – it was just like you, Molly, in your wedding dress – and it spoke every word that the man was saying straight to

me.' Molly and I glanced at each other with a look of
wonder and thankfulness in our eyes. For so long we had
been very sorrowful that we had failed our Lord in
speaking of his love, but this proved to be the start of a
completely changed relationship.

There was now a request for prayer every time we
visited, and when ultimately Grandad was let out of
hospital for some three weeks, we were able to have
prayer times whenever we met him at home until his
dying day. Furthermore, the evidence of a changed life
was in changed behaviour. The ward-sister commented
on the sudden disappearance of Grandad's grumpiness
and frustration, and wanted to know what had happened to make such a difference. Suddenly he had
become a joy to nurse, because he had Christ in his life.
After our years of failing to share Christ with Grandad,
suddenly our sorrow was turned into joy. God had done
directly by his Spirit and through this mysterious messenger what we had been unable to do. Though we are
called to have a purpose in people's eternal destiny
through our believing prayer, ultimately it is God's responsibility to break through and to reveal what no
human agency can declare to another person.

Molly and I realised how stupid we were. We had
allowed our anxiety concerning Grandad's physical illness to cloud our faith completely. If he had died and
someone had asked us if he had died in faith, we should
have said, 'No, we failed to share our Saviour with him.'
What we ought to have said was: 'Yes, of course he died
in faith, we have prayed believing for him for five years,
and though we were not given the opportunity to give an
answer for the hope that is in us, surely God will have
broken through to his life somehow.'

In preparing for a life of ministry, I had been terrified
that I should be guilty of many and massive failures.
Unlike a surgeon, whose mistake is obvious if he ampu-
tates the wrong limb by mistake, I felt that I might on
many occasions fail to share Jesus with another person,

or I might put off visiting them in hospital, and then find that they died before I had opportunity to do my duty. All this burden of fear was taken away from me when I realised how marvellously God had worked in answer to our prayers. Here was a deathbed repentance, but we were given sufficient time to see the evidence of a changed life and to be sure that the repentance was genuine. We were thrilled to think of the fruitfulness of that clergyman's ministry, who will never know this side of the grave that while he spoke at that routine hospital ward service an angelic visitation took place and that there was rejoicing in heaven over a sinner who repented. God tells us through the prophet: 'My word . . . shall not return to me empty, but it shall accomplish that which I purpose, and prosper in the thing for which I sent it' (Isa 55:11).

The faith for deathbed situations which that incident stirred has been valuable throughout years of ministry. Notably, when caring nurses have attempted to bar entry to a seemingly unconscious patient, out of concern for the person in their care, I have had faith to persist with my request to meet the dying person, aware that I might be the deathbed messenger who will be the answer to the prayers of believing relatives or friends. Time and time again the word of God has penetrated the apparent unconsciousness and through a squeeze of the hand, or some other sign, indicated without speech that the message of God's love was heard and understood. The familiar words of the Lord's Prayer or the twenty-third psalm frequently brought an identifiable movement of the lips, and I could only trust there was a sympathetic acceptance of the message.

Sometimes there is a deathbed struggle. I remember visiting a man with my rector, Geoffrey Shaw. His wife was a Scottish lady of delightful, trusting faith who used to read the Scriptures to him every night and prayed for him every day of their marriage. Unfortunately he was someone who had been let down very badly by other

Christians in a business venture, and for years he had been unable to forgive them or God for his own severe financial loss. Geoffrey had visited him regularly in his final illness, but every time came up against firm opposition whenever the man was challenged to trust in God. 'No, no, no,' he would cry between gritted teeth as Geoffrey pleaded with him to open his heart to Christ and to forgiveness. His enfeebled hands gripped tightly so that the flesh went white, and the skin stretched over his knuckles. Every week he was consistent in his vehemence against turning to Christ.

I was enormously impressed with the way Geoffrey pleaded, gently cajoled, and firmly warned this reluctant believer of the consequences of dying without Christ. He persisted far beyond my ability to cope with the rejection of our ministry. The day finally came when it was evident that the end was near. Geoffrey used the words of the Lord's Prayer and lovingly encouraged the man to humble himself and go back on his previous unmovable attitude in rejecting Christ. He urged him to join in the words, making it a final surrender to the Father's love. As I prayed in silence Geoffrey said the words of the Lord's Prayer out loud, and there was a movement of the lips and a barely audible rehearsal of the familiar words. He closed his eyes and died with a peaceful smile that remained set in his features.

This is the truly sensitive area in such ministry – the handling of any information about the life expectancy of the person to whom one is ministering. Fortunately there is today a much greater openness and willingness for the whole family unit to share the prognosis of the doctors and to face up to the possibility of death together.

One of the biggest mistakes I made early in my ministry was to be a party to the conniving deception of a family who did their utmost to keep the truth from their dying loved one. John was a former guard on the Southern Railway who in his retirement years found Christ as his Saviour. Soon after becoming a member of his local church he was admitted to hospital, where a colostomy operation was performed. As he returned home, the doctors told his wife that they thought he had only two weeks or so to live, and on the strength of that forecast I promised to visit every day. Three months later I was still visiting.

For John the process of dying was miserably and excruciatingly painful. His wife, so certain of his impending death, had already got rid of all his clothes and his shoes and maintained a charade of bonhomie and small-talk, never able to look death in the eye with her partner. Having agreed to her request not to tell him the true nature of his condition, I was bound by my promise to her and would not have been in a position to help her in her bereavement if I had failed to observe her wish. His doctor was unwilling to step up the dose of painkilling drug, and poor John writhed in agony night and day, week after week. One morning he pleaded with me: 'If only someone would tell me the truth.' In words that I cannot now recall, I was somehow able to keep my promise to his wife and yet to make it quite plain to him that he was on the verge of death – indeed within half an hour from that sharing of truth he was at peace.

I vowed never again to fall into the same trap, and though it was possible to keep the trust of John's wife, I feel responsible for many hours of apparently fruitless pain. If I had persuaded both John and his wife to face up to the truth of his illness, I could have counselled him to meet death with Christian hope and I could have helped her to accept bereavement with the help of God's comfort. In the end, both of these realities were experienced and over the period of John's suffering, his wife did come to terms with his passing.

It is pointless to evade the issue of death. Whether or not someone has a 'terminal' illness it is still possible to be killed in a car smash on the way to hospital, and because we all have the terminal illness of sin to contend with, we need to be ready every moment of every day to face our maker. This was illustrated vividly in the case of two young people who on completely different occasions attended meetings at which I was speaking. One of these meetings was at my old school in Dorking. It was a small-scale evangelistic meeting to tie in with one of Billy Graham's visits to London, and though there is always urgency in preaching the gospel, it did not seem that with a company of young people present there was any desperate need to prepare them for imminent death and ultimate judgment. However, in the course of the meeting a definite constraint came upon me to urge each one present to be ready to meet the Lord at any moment. At the time I was fearful lest I had spoken too strongly, but a few days later the schoolteacher who arranged the meeting wrote to me with the shattering news that one of the fifth formers present had taken her usual bus home after the meeting, and in crossing the road at the other end of the journey had been knocked down by a passing car and was killed outright.

A similar urgency came upon me when I was preaching at a university mission at Ibadan, Nigeria. It seemed that though there was a great response to the gospel, in that thousands of students attended the meetings, many were going away without responding to the gospel. I felt impelled to ask the question: 'Which of you, having woken up to each morning of your life, can be sure that you will wake up tomorrow?' I then felt that this sounded almost like a threat which might put a wrong pressure on those who were listening. However, I thought of how George Whitefield, the eighteenth-century evangelist, used to tell his hearers of the blind man who was walking, without any sense of impending danger, to the edge of a precipice. 'Turn back,' a man who saw what was about to happen shouted, 'turn back before it's too late. You are walking to your death.' Whitefield told his hearers that the man was not threatening death, but warning the blind man in love, so that he might turn back and change his course before it was too late. I likewise made this clear to the audience of Nigerian students.

The next day was Sunday, and outside Kuti Hall a crowd of people were standing and staring towards the window. In typical English style I joined the crowd and looked. There was in fact nothing to be seen, so after some minutes I asked what everyone was waiting for. 'Oh, haven't you heard? One of the students died in his sleep last night.' It turned out that he had been suffering from a previously unrecognised epileptic condition, and without any warning had died without waking up to another day. He had given his life to Christ the night before. The impact on the campus was profound, and many professed faith during the final day of the mission. Only eternity will tell how many of those were genuinely believing rather than just frightened people seeking an 'insurance policy'.

12   Father Tom

The new young curate with the gleaming white, wrong-way round collar which was making angry red marks around his inexperienced neck, was sent to visit two chair-bound, arthritic, elderly sisters, who hired the top floor of a smart nursing home in Woking. It was his first call on these ladies, so he was unknown to them and also to the Spanish maid who opened the front door.

I was beginning to discover the hazards of parish visiting. It may seem simple to pay a pastoral call on the elderly and infirm. But as soon as she saw me, the maid slammed the door in my face and fled upstairs. I was left wondering if I was welcome, if it was a convenient time to call, and if the maid had understood my explanation of the purpose of my call. I waited and waited – wondering.

Just as I was about to leave the doorstep in order to make a more profitable call, the door opened again, and the same Spanish maid looked at me open-mouthed; then she slammed the door shut in my face a second time, and again I heard her footsteps as she rushed up the staircase inside the flat. Not a word had passed between us, so I remained there, more perplexed than ever. Lord, do I stick it out and find an opportunity here, or is it just a waste of time?,' I prayed inwardly.

After a further lengthy wait, during which I resolved to gain access if at all possible, the maid again opened the front door and beckoned me in. She led me to the top floor and into the presence of the two sweetest, most uncomplaining, truly believing sisters it has ever been my privilege to meet. They provided for me the first vivid illustration of how old age can offer one loss after another: the loss of home and of health, of movement and of independent choice and action. The world's horizons can narrow down to the four walls of a rented room, where one's well-being depends on the kindness and attention of people paid to cope with the necessities of a limited and handicapped existence. In such circumstances the inner attitude counts for so much, and the acceptance of – or the rebellion against – one's destiny can make anyone's home either a prison-house of frustration or a cosy nest within which there is security, sustenance and peace. It was said of two prisoners: 'Two men look out through the same bars: one sees the mud and one sees the stars.' Both were subject to the same hardships, but only one developed inner stress and exposed himself to disease. The other found inspiration in the stars and his attitude to imprisonment was transformed.

These two ladies, who in a bygone era would have been described as 'gentlefolk', had the most remarkable ability to accept pain and handicap and to be positively cheerful in their affliction. Speaking of the human body and its frailty, St Paul likened it to a 'tent' that is to be destroyed. He said, 'Here indeed we groan, and long to put on our heavenly dwelling' (2 Cor 5:2). He knew that 'Though our outer nature is wasting away, our inner nature is being renewed every day. For this slight momentary affliction is preparing for us an eternal weight of glory' (2 Cor 4:16–17).

These two saints were confidently 'in the heavenly places in Christ Jesus' (Eph 2:6) and the physical restriction of their earthly circumstances did not narrow their vision of God. My first encounter with them was a hilariously enjoyable time as they narrated the background to the waiting game I had been forced to play on the front doorstep. Apparently the Spanish maid had rushed upstairs and had told the ladies that there was a little boy to see them. My diminutive stature and youthful appearance had caused her to take many years off my age. This was partly because I had been wearing a university scarf tossed nonchalantly around my neck, covering up the shining new clerical collar. The two sisters had assumed that I was one of the local wolf cubs who regularly helped them by fetching books from the library. They sent the maid downstairs, asking her to show the 'little boy' up to their room. Imagine their consternation when having spotted my dog collar she came dashing back again to tell them in broken English 'The little boy's a Father.' 'Well, fetch him up,' they said, wondering who to expect.

We all laughed at the misunderstanding, but I was able to share with the ladies that in a literal sense the maid's description was true. Our first child, Charis, had been born that very week in Woking Maternity Hospital. I was Father Tom to the most beautiful little scrap of humanity with the loudest screams in the ward. 'You can tell she's a preacher's daughter,' the ward-sister said, 'she yells louder than any other baby in the hospital!'

Although Molly and I were thrilled with our new status as parents, we look back in amazement as we realise what little instruction we had been given as we entered Christian parenthood. The hospital was excellent in describing bath-time techniques, and in demonstrating what to do with baby-grows, baby buds and baby powder, not to mention nappies, Milton, milk and magnesia. But no one told us how to pray ourselves into glad parenthood. No one warned us of the total disruption of every aspect of life – days off, visits to parents, evenings out, getting to church meetings and Sunday services, holidays, sleep at nights, shopping, loading the car, etc.

As we found ourselves in touch with many young families in the parish, we soon came to understand why so many parents of small children quickly become disillusioned with their role. The chores of life predominate, and some wives, swamped by motherhood, almost deliberately give up being sexually attractive as wives to their partners. Some men find excuses not to pull their weight in the home and become absent fathers. Lacking intellectual stimulation, clever parents become consumed with the trivialities of nappy talk, and the baby is blamed for bringing a blight on the marriage. Instead of the child bringing parents together in a new bond of love and care, it is blamed for interfering with pleasures and hobbies and even in Christian homes becomes the source of division and disintegration in family life.

Molly and I were determined not to fall into this trap. From the start we wanted to give thanks to God for the miracle of a new life. Because Molly had worked for so many years among severely mentally handicapped people in long-stay mental hospitals, she could hardly believe that we should be privileged to have an undamaged child. For her, mental and physical disorder were the norm, and the gift of a 'normal' baby seemed almost too much to hope for. But when Charis was born, her very name telling that we counted her 'a gift of grace', we determined to view her upbringing, and that of any other children we might be given, as both a joy and a solemn responsibility given by God.

It was only twenty months later that our second child, Rachel, was born. Again we were taken by surprise, because no one had prepared us properly for parenthood. In our ignorance we assumed that to have two babies close together would double the workload and cause double the trouble. We were in danger of taking a very negative view of family life and the bringing up of children – an attitude which we criticised in other people. Instead we found that Rachel fitted happily into the routine already established for Charis. In fact, the two little girls gave us double the joy as we all grew together in God's love.

A biblical view of family life does not allow for parental tantrums over the hard work and sacrifice involved in parenthood. Nor does it allow parents to forsake their charge, surrendering the delicate task of godly training to child minders, play-group leaders, or friends. The Bible emphasis is on teaching, training, instructing. The child in godly Jewish families is the child of the covenant, and believing Jewish parents know their covenant duties:

> And these words which I command you this day shall be upon your heart; and you shall teach them diligently to your children, and shall talk of them when you sit in your house, and when you walk by the way, and when you lie down, and when you rise. And you shall bind them as a sign upon your hand, and they shall be as frontlets between your eyes. And you shall write them on the doorposts of your house and on your gates. (Deut 6:6–9)

In New Testament days, the leaders of the early church had to be those who 'hold firm to the sure word as taught . . . able to give instruction in sound doctrine and also to confute those who contradict it' (Tit 1:9). So Timothy, though relatively young in years, was notably well prepared for the office of bishop in the church because he was 'from childhood . . . acquainted with the sacred writings' (2 Tim 3:15); and clearly the fact that he had both a believing mother and grandmother (2 Tim 1:5) meant that he was taught from the cradle by these godly women.

Far from opting out of parental responsibilities, Molly and I saw the opportunity to lead our children to personal faith in Christ at the earliest age possible, and looked on the chance of teaching them as much as we could in the few, rapidly passing years available to us as a rare privilege. The first task given to Peter in the threefold recommissioning of John 21, after the resurrection appearance by the Sea of Galilee, was 'Feed my lambs' (John 21:15). Who knows how the child in our care might grow up for God and be of immense importance in his strategic purposes. Not everyone can be a Hudson Taylor, a William Temple or a Billy Graham, but any child in our care may have the potential of being that significant for God.

Our technique was relaxed rather than disciplinarian. Night-time prayers and reading provided the key time together, as we were not happy with the concept of a rigidly imposed family prayer time. We have known so many homes where the ritual of family prayers has not been matched by loving Christian relationships, and the last thing we wanted was to create a rebellion against imposed religion as had happened in my own father's Strict Baptist upbringing. Our more informal pattern offered our children the chance of developing their own private discipline of prayer, which I am sure they fail at as often as we do ourselves, but the balance between corporate family prayers led by a parent and a personal devotional pattern for which the child is responsible from an early age gives room for their own spiritual development and growth.

Because of this relaxed programme, it became natural to share together the big matters and the urgent problems in prayer. Charis was in and out of hospital as a small child, and her health was a regular subject of united prayer. Rachel developed a fear of ghosts and witches because of the literature she was expected to read at school as a very small child, and every fear was immediately dissipated as we had a bedtime prayer against Satan's working.

Our children could be involved in ministry to people who stayed in our home for extended counselling and prayer. During the time that we worked in London with IVF among university students, Charis and Rachel became used to relating to house-guests who were much older than themselves. However, by the time we moved to the Midlands to join the staff of Birmingham Cathedral, ministry in our home had taken on a new dimension. On one occasion a man who claimed to have asked thirty-three evil spirits into his life was screaming and rampaging in our lounge as a group of Christians prayed for him. Neighbours in several houses on either side of ours were disturbed and hung out of their windows, wondering if someone was being murdered. We realised that Charis and Rachel could not fail to have been woken up themselves, and when we asked in the morning we found that they had been praying upstairs in their bedroom as we had been ministering downstairs in the early hours of the morning.

At other times the whole family ministered to those who lived in our home, sometimes for months at a time. At a very tender age the girls were adept at phoning for an ambulance and then contacting the casualty department of a local hospital to warn of the arrival of someone who had taken an overdose of drugs. Once, when I was involved in a mission abroad, a member of our congregation rang up to tell the vicarage family that their baby had suddenly died – another in the statistics of the inexplicable cot-death syndrome. Rachel was aged just thirteen at the time, and knew that it was not enough just to take a message and that some ministry was required. She searched around, wondering what to say, and then her eyes fell on a card pinned on the notice board just above the telephone. It was an extended message of comfort, and as she read it out to the distraught, bereaved mother, she said: 'This is just what you need to hear' – and it was.

A big day for the girls was when they had tea with Cliff Richard. He was singing and giving his testimony at a packed-out rally in Birmingham Cathedral. In the course of the evening he said that it was just four years since he had first given his life to Christ. I noticed Rachel counting on her fingers. She leant across to me and in a stage whisper announced: 'I've been a Christian twice as long, Daddy.'

These stories feature Rachel because surrender to the Lord was for her both harder and more measurable than it was for Charis. Charis had always been the archetypal 'good little girl'. She had always wanted to please, and in her early days never seemed to have a mind in rebellion to Christ. Rachel, on the other hand, had a mind of her own, and like many a second child had to make her presence felt. At the nightly prayer time we would sometimes put forward a gentle challenge to Christian commitment, using the words of the old chorus: 'Come into my heart, come into my heart, come into my heart Lord Jesus. Come in today, come in to stay, come into my heart Lord Jesus.' We knew Charis had prayed the prayer, and we would ask Rachel if she was ready to pray it too. 'No,' she would reply gruffly, 'No!' So we left it. But one day, at the age of three, she was suddenly quite definite. It was her day, and eight years later at the Cliff Richard rally she could remember it clearly.

Just about this time, Timothy our son was born. He was also no slouch in growing up to Christian commitment. One Easter Sunday I was preaching at the morning Family Service, making up, in the visual age, the fictitious front page of the *Jerusalem Echo* as it might have appeared at the time of Jesus. The last gap to be filled in carried a picture of Holman Hunt's 'Light of the World' – inserted with massive disregard of the historical timescale. I could see that young Timothy's eyes were as wide as saucers all the way through. Also only three years old, but God was speaking to him, and without hesitancy or subsequent doubt he prayed the prayer of commitment to Jesus in a three year old's way that morning.

Each child has to become his or her own person, so each must tell their own tale of their growing towards faith in Christ. What Molly and I are quite sure about as parents is that the family unit is the key unit in God's plan for human community and growth. No other human activity, work or hobby, secular duty or church responsibility, must be allowed to destroy family bonds. The brief time that our children have for growth and development is over so quickly, and too many parents allow the time for godly instruction and spiritual influence to pass without using the opportunity to the full. If we are asked for any secret to the remarkable harmony and love we have known as a Christian family, we should sum it up in a motto that Molly and I have often used both in discipline and mutual encouragement. It is this: 'We all love Jesus, don't we?' If there is any query about behaviour or duty or family style, we remind each other that we are all 'children of the covenant'. We have all received God's personal promise to us. We are all committed to him as he has committed himself to us, so as a family we live the Jesus way and serve one another in love. Of course, we often fail, but when we do we can start again. We can forgive each other again, as God has forgiven us, and we can know security with each other in the bond of family love.

13   Opportunity knocks

'He who believes will not be in haste.' I remember these
words shining out of Isaiah 28 as though they had been
written in gold. It was around the time of sorting out my
call to the ministry, and the passage from Isaiah came up
in the course of reading right through the Bible following
a scheme of systematic study. I had never consciously
read the verse before, but it had more than usual significance that morning. With so many people to see, and so
many decisions to make, I was tempted to hurry at
everything rather than live by faith, allowing the purpose
of providence to work out.

The same verse came up again in a book I was reading
later that morning, and somebody quoted it during a
prayer time in the lunch-hour. 'Three times Lord,' I
thought, 'okay, I've got the message – I do understand.'
Somehow the same verse cropped up again during the
afternoon and then because it was a Wednesday, the one
day in the week when we had Choral Evensong in
Chapel, I went for some peace and rest from these
emphatic communications from God. I hoped to hide in
the choir stalls, where I had many years of experience of
coping with services without such incisive communica-
tion from the mouth of the Lord! I was glancing through
the tenor part of the setting of the Magnificat we were
going to sing and hardly heard the Old Testament lesson
announced. However, after a few minutes, guilt set in
and I put the copy down on to the choir stall and listened
with at least half an ear to the reading of Scripture. 'He
who believes will not be in haste.' The words had now

become arrows, and they pierced afresh to my innermost being.

To a young Christian the remarkable coincidence of some words from one chapter coming with such peculiar intensity five times in one day was an inescapable sign that God was guiding through his word.

Years later the story had its sequel. Rachel, two foot nothing tall, was standing on tiptoe peering out of the back-room window of our little terraced house in North London. Her big brown eyes grew bigger and rounder as she saw two fierce-looking men leap across our fence, the front one with a hammer in his hand, to find a getaway route from the house they had been burgling. 'Mummy, mummy,' she cried and Molly dashed to the back door and slammed it shut and then flung herself at the kitchen window to keep them from breaking through. This in itself was a miracle, in that on so many days at this time she had been laid out unconscious by a mystery illness which the most careful examination at a top London hospital could not diagnose. The burglar had been terrorising the neighbourhood for some time.

The pressure of illness and these unpleasant experiences, together with the inadequacy of the local medical care, were pushing us to the point of giving up the student work which we were enjoying so much. And then one afternoon, as I was driving home from a conference on the outskirts of London, I switched on the car radio and heard the words, 'He who believes will not be in haste.' The sing-song voice of a cathedral canon brought the words home as vividly as that day more than ten years before when the same passage of Scripture found its allotted place in a Wednesday's lectionary. It only came up once every two years, and I doubt if I had turned on the radio for Cathedral Evensong for weeks if not months. All the lessons of God's guidance and care came flooding back. All the mistrust and unbelief was admitted. 'Lord,' I prayed, 'you've got an answer. I can't see what it will be, but I do know we're meant to hang on.'

In fact the answer came the very next weekend. A Christian doctor came up to me in the church in Hampstead where we worshipped on the Sundays I was not preaching at student meetings. 'Tom', he said, 'I've been thinking about Molly's problem. We don't know what it is medically, but I wonder if it would be a help if I took her on to my books.' 'But we're miles out of your area,' I replied, 'How can we possibly ask you to keep an eye on her when I'm away so much?' 'I believe we're meant to do it,' he said, 'and it will be all right.' So we stayed on in London and the coincidence of God's intervention was confirmed. (It was only years later in Birmingham that the rest of the difficulty was discovered and some necessary surgery was performed.)

Signs of loving care like this are vital when the way gets hard. When things go wrong we could so easily blame ourselves for being in the wrong place and for missing God's will, but through unmistakable guidance he makes it clear that we are in the right place at the right time. 'Make thy way plain before my face' was the prayer I made when surrendering to ordination, and it has been consistently answered.

Another time when we needed very special leading involved the question of moving from one parish to another. I had been working for just over a year in a parish in Woking, and was still in spiritual nappies as far as the ministry was concerned, when the bombshell came that the vicar, Geoff Shaw, was leaving. Molly and I felt that we had so much more to learn from him and his wife, and had been so totally happy learning to serve with them, and it seemed that the bottom had fallen out of our world. Very quickly he asked us to go with him to Sussex by the sea, but that seemed easier said than done.

We cried out to God about it, and we searched the Bible, and we looked out for messages from heaven, but nothing came. Not even, 'He who believes will not be in haste'! We consulted the bishop, but to say he was not impressed with the idea of a move is an understatement. I went to two respected friends and they gave completely conflicting advice. One said, 'Tom, this is your chance of a lifetime – come and be *my* curate!' He meant it very kindly, but for me the real question was whether to go with Geoff or to stay amidst the pines of Surrey. The other man, a dear godly retired bishop, said, 'Tom, I believe you should go. Whatever you have learnt from a man settled in a parish is good to know. But see him in a completely new situation, with a totally new set of people, and you will learn from his mistakes there as well as from his successes here.' But still there was no word from God himself. The ultimatum came. Geoff had come to the limit of his patience as we delayed over weeks and months. 'I must know by next Monday,' he said, 'There is someone else who is keen to come, but I'll stick by my word as I made you the first offer. But Monday is the deadline.'

Our problem was not that we did not want to go. In fact we were suspicious of our own motives because the call was so attractive. Who would not want to minister at a glorious new parish church right on the seafront of St Leonard's on Sea? Who would not be challenged by the thought of ministering to seaside crowds, with unexpected notables in the congregation Sunday by Sunday every summer? Who would not be intrigued by preaching from a beautiful Galilean boat pulpit made by craftsmen beside the Sea of Galilee, in a style and tradition unchanged since the days of Jesus himself? What landlubber would not be attracted to life by the sea? Every motivation seemed to have an element of vanity in it, and we distrusted our own thoughts on the matter. But we had a deadline. We needed to hear God's voice and to know God's call.

It happened that the final weekend for decision was one when we were due to be away in Sussex, and so on the Sunday morning we drove across to spy out the land at St Leonard's Parish Church. A most amazing sequence of events ensued. The curate whom we were due to replace saw Molly and I in the congregation and knew that we were looking to God for help with our decision. As he began to read the Old Testament lesson he prayed to the Lord, 'Please Lord, speak to Tom and Molly through this passage and make your will plain to them.' It was the story of Joshua and Caleb and the other men going to spy out the Promised Land. We did not apply it to ourselves, it seemed to be just another reading from Scripture on just another Sunday at just another service of Morning Prayer. But God had other ideas. He spoke to the preacher as he sat on the clergy stall. 'You've got to preach on that passage,' he said. The thought came ringing as a conviction in the preacher's mind. 'But Lord, I can't. You know I can't preach extemporary sermons, and in any case I've got all my notes clearly written out here in front of me.' This debate continued in his mind not only through all the Old Testament reading, but it completely wrecked the Te Deum for him as well! The poor preacher was a visitor from a missionary society who had hoped for a quiet Sunday preachment and had certainly not allowed for this uncomfortable divine intervention.

Molly and I continued through the service blissfully unaware of any pattern of divine providence being worked out. Then the sermon came, and the preacher was obedient. 'The oracles are dumb to those who disobey,' the old saying goes, but that morning the preacher was the conveyer of oracles from God to us. In fact the sermon was the worst I have ever heard preached, and the preacher had a true estimate of himself when he told the Lord that he could not preach extemporary sermons. But all through the sermon one word came rattling through like machinegun fire. 'Opportunity, opportunity, opportunity, opportunity . . .' The point he was making from that Old Testament passage was that there were two sorts of men who went to spy out the land with

Joshua. There were those who saw only giants in the land, obstacles to the way ahead, and who turned back with doubt in their hearts. There were others who saw beyond the giants to the opportunity in the new land which God was giving to his people, and they went ahead and came back from spying out the land with the fruit of the land in their hands and with the encouragement to trust God's promise on their lips.

After that sermon I felt that if the whole bench of bishops was opposed to us moving to St Leonard's, they and any other giants in the land would in this instance have to give way to a clear call from God. Talking to the preacher after the service the whole story of his inner struggle came out, and we could only wonder.

It turned out that we needed this degree of confidence, because when we said 'yes' to Geoff Shaw the next morning we little realised that times of testing and trial were ahead in a way that we had never known before. The afflictions were small compared to other people's suffering, but they brought a new dimension of life to us. Indeed, we could have wondered if we had taken a wrong course and these troubles were signs of God's chastening on our lives had it not been for such a special sense of God's leading to that particular place.

I remember a dreadful Monday morning. Our guard should have been up, but the enemy got in with a blow below the belt. That is not to say that we blame all the trouble in our lives on to the devil. We have human responsibility for wrong actions and wrong attitudes that lead to trouble and strife, but it is plain that Satan is the author of trouble and confusion in the world, and that bitterness and jealousy and selfish ambition in our hearts are 'earthly, unspiritual, devilish' rather than 'heavenly, spiritual, godly' aspects of our lives (cf. Jas 3:14 ff.). Just as the devil got at Jesus in the wilderness at a point of hunger and self-questioning, so he gets at us at our points of human frailty. Monday was our day off, normally kept for the family as a special day together. But we had hardly washed the marmalade off the breakfast plates when things started to go wrong. I said quite innocently (but on reflection quite selfishly), 'I'll just go and finish some letters, Molly, and then we can have a day together in the garden, there's so much to do.' 'No, you won't,' Molly replied, 'You'll go straight into the garden now. This is our day off, and it's certainly not the day for parish work.' 'But I won't enjoy the day until I clear my desk,' I pleaded. 'No, you promised that Monday was our day off, and if it's our day off there's no time for letters.' 'But it won't take me five minutes,' I argued. Voices were raised, wills asserted, doors slammed, and in place of order there was confusion, and instead of peace there was strife.

After a short time I emerged shamefaced saying: 'I'm sorry Molly, I shouldn't have shouted. I'll go into the garden now.' 'No, you won't,' she said, 'Finish your letters and then we can do the garden.' 'No,' I said, 'I'll go into the garden now, this minute. That's what you wanted, and that's what I'll do. After all it is our day off!' And with determined stride I went through the kitchen and into the back garden to get in among the weeds. Still annoyed at my ungracious attempt to be gracious, Molly went into the front garden, to complete the picture of disharmony. Amidst all this, Charis, our two year old, was scampering in and out, busy with her playthings and seemingly quite unconcerned at this unusual altercation between her parents.

Then the postman called, and with the front door and back door open, a tremendous gust of wind slammed shut the inner door of the bungalow just as Charis passed through clutching an armful of dolls. The door trapped her finger, and rushing to her screams the family was united again in a child's suffering.

The frenzied dash to the hospital with tyres screaming, horn blasting, and total disregard of prescribed speed limits proved only the troubled impatience of anxious human hearts. Every accident is only one of scores of

96

others in our accident-prone world, and together with all the other accidents of that Monday morning we ended up in the 'Wait Here' section of the hospital's casualty department.

'Why did we hurry?' we thought. 'We've only jumped the queue of someone else's suffering.' But then our turn came and our fears proved well founded. The tip of the finger had been taken off and was not to be found in the makeshift bandage we had put together with the nearest tea-towel. The bare bone was exposed, and only X-rays could show the full extent of the damage. But the surgeon on duty was encouraging. 'Amputation to the first joint may be necessary, but let's take a positive view,' he said. 'Go back home, and if you find the tip of the finger bring it in and we'll sew it on in any case if we can. And we'll persevere,' he added. 'We'll not give up easily.'

Arriving home some six hours after the accident, the missing finger tip was soon found, mixed up with chips of paint from the door and dust from the floor. An unpromising piece of flesh at the best of times! And at that point God's messenger arrived. Bill Read, then the vicar of Bridlington, and an old friend, arrived at the moment of need. Human anxiety and fear were turned into prayer; selfish remorse and guilt were turned into repentance. And basically we knew that prayer, together with the needle and thread and the surgeon's skill working on that tiny piece of flesh on a toddler's finger, would all combine for good effect.

The surgeon was in fact the father of one of our young people at church and we sensed a special care for Charis in his tone. He had a theory that to carry on with such a surgical repair job beyond the point of seeming hopelessness often led to good results in the end, as the healing powers of the body took their full course. So it was to be with Charis, and we have been many times grateful that a surgeon who himself had suffered seriously from exposure to the bitter cold of the North Sea waters as a baled-out fighter pilot in the war, was the man on duty that day. He had proved in his own body the remarkable powers of healing and recovery.

But our lessons were not ended yet. Only when we had experienced the strain created by the long visiting hours allowed to small children did we realise the sacrifices made by parents who had children suffering from long-term illnesses. Only when our own little girl screamed in agonising pain could we understand the helplessness of those who watch their loved ones suffer. No one had told us how much harder it is to see your own children bearing pain than it is to suffer yourself. Like most parents we had on occasions been driven to frustration by one of the babies crying, particularly that incessant fractious wailing at times of illness. It is easy to condemn those who resort to baby battering, but because it is so hard for the adult to put himself into the position of the helpless baby it is sometimes hard to sympathise with the distressed baby. Not so the older child. The more it develops, the more love grows and the harder it is for the caring parent to stand aside and see its pain.

The grief of a bereaved parent is beyond our ken, though more than once our family has looked death in the eye. Charis was in and out of hospital seven times in as many years when she was small, and on one occasion she had been rushed breathless into a moisturising tent. We were given no guarantee by the medical staff that she would recover. On one occasion we were told that it was unlikely that she would survive until the morning. Despite the gravity of the situation, we were amazed how peacefully we were able to pray that night and say, 'The Lord gave and the Lord has taken away.' Of course, it was easy to say the words, and had she died there would have been depths of grief which we were not called to plumb. None the less, our testimony is that God gave remarkable peace, and an ability to surrender a very precious life, when circumstances were black indeed.

With Rachel the praying was less easy. In her teenage years she suffered a whole year of serious illness at a crucial time in her schooling. Though expected to recover in a matter of weeks from this mystery virus, over a period of months she literally wasted away before our eyes. Unable to endure even the weight of a sheet on her body, she sat night after night in a reclining chair in front of the fire, struggling even for a moment's sleep. By that time our church was experienced in praying for the sick, and we had many testimonies of answered prayer and of some quite dramatic instances of healing. Equally we knew of other people for whom we had prayed who had died rapidly though peacefully. It was so much easier to be the minister of healing to others than it was to be the 'wounded healer' experiencing months of seemingly unanswered prayer. If anything the pressure of this was more on Rachel than on ourselves. She so much wanted to be the answer to people's believing prayer, and could hardly face the disappointment of reporting that she felt little better, indeed probably somewhat worse each time they came to pray. She almost dreaded the visits of some well-meaning Christian friends who did not wish to be accusatory, but who gave the impression by their disappointment at Rachel's lack of improvement that she was herself letting them down or in some way not co-operating with their prayers. This made her feel burdened and threatened rather than encouraged and uplifted, and taught us all lessons about how to cope with the problem of persevering through a period when prayer seems to be unanswered.

Again, it was the timing of God's answer to our prayers that was important. The turning point for Rachel came when I knew that humanly we could take no more. In the midst of busy ministry, with continuing prayer for healing for others, and many evidences of God's power at work to restore and mend lives in answer to believing prayer, we still had no evidence of the healing of Rachel's long-standing illness. One night, however, I arrived home somewhere near midnight and went into the room where Rachel was keeping her nightly vigil, sitting up in a chair, unable to sleep or rest. We prayed together as on many other occasions, but that night I knew that there was a difference of quality in our praying. There was authority, there was an amazing sense of God's holy presence, and there was peace that the transformation was about to take place. In this particular instance the change was not due to any special medication. The condition was still a complete mystery to the doctors who examined her. But the suddenness of the improvement was dramatic and spoke to us of God's powerful sovereign intervention.

We are still left asking why the illness continued for so many months before believing prayer was answered. We can only say that had the prayer not continued for so long and had the situation not seemed so hopeless humanly speaking, we would not have given all the glory to God for such a marvellous deliverance. The whole experience was a test of our faith as well as a character building process for Rachel.

14 The Lord our healer

'Does your husband ever beat you?' the earnest lady consultant asked my wife at the Royal Free Hospital in London. It was a question asked out of frustration, because not one of many X-rays or the medical tests showed the reason for Molly's periodic bursts of agonising pain. The tests could not confirm her preferred diagnosis, even though, as she said: 'It's the clearest case of gall stones I've ever seen.' She lacked the nerve to act on intuition and experience in the absence of any scientific information to confirm her diagnosis. In the circumstances it was quite reasonable to ask this young wife with a haggard, pain-drawn face, whether her reverend husband regularly indulged in wife-beating! 'No,' she answered firmly, 'he has never hit me since we first knew each other at the age of five. I used to kick his shins when I was little, but he is not a wife-beater.'

In the healing process it was necessary to find out all the facts. Did this woman need the surgeon's scalpel? Could she be healed by drugs? Or was the pain just in her mind? Should a marriage guidance counsellor be brought in? Or was there a deeper spiritual problem for which prayer was needed? Perhaps this pain, which for years had been spoken of as 'migraine of the stomach', could be the expression of some inner resistance to being a clergyman's wife. It could simply represent inner tension – the hangover from experiencing the break-up of her home during childhood. It might be accounted for by some inner physical disorder, but if nothing showed up in tests or X-rays it could be due to some other factor in her life. It was certainly right to ask the questions.

Nowadays, many Christians have been led by God into a ministry of spiritual and inner healing which could have been pertinent in this situation. Molly could have been referred to a psychiatrist or a psychotherapist for extended counselling or drug therapy. However, after ten more years of incapacitating pain, it was found that she had gall stones. They still did not show up on X-rays, but a surgeon in Birmingham was prepared to back his hunch by taking out the gall bladder, and there were the stones! In this instance counselling was not the answer. Prayer helped, of course, but the surgeon's knife provided the answer.

Some years later, Molly's health was again in question. This time it was the scourge of so many silent sufferers – back trouble. Years of constant pain and sleepless, drug-ged nights, following the birth of Rachel, our second child, caused us to query the wisdom of having any more children. Then with a sense of God's call, though, humanly speaking, taking a calculated risk, Timothy was born. 'Is there anything wrong?' the nurse asked, when Molly's blood pressure went sky high after childbirth. 'Are you worrying about anything?' 'The only thing I'm worrying about,' Molly replied, 'is that you won't let me go home today.' 'That's fine then,' the nurse said, 'I'll see what they say.' 'They' said Molly could go home, but she was to remain as quiet as possible in the hope that her blood pressure would lower. But it didn't.

Just at that time Jean Darnall, the American teacher and healer, was giving a series of evening talks at Bir-mingham Cathedral. 'Do come and see Molly,' I asked, 'she's still got high blood pressure and her back feels as though it's broken in half.' She came to our home and prayed, believing for God's healing. It was quite clear that she was confident about dealing with the high blood pressure, but had no leading at all about the crippling condition of Molly's back.

For months we had been learning to live with this handicap of pain, though it was not easy to have our faith tested over such a long period of time. Although at that stage the high blood pressure seemed to be a secondary problem, it was certainly not the reason why we had asked Jean to come for special prayer. Jean was so confident that the Lord had intervened, that Molly felt able to dispense with her medication. Her blood pressure was being checked regularly at post-natal visits by the district midwife, and sure enough, the readings were within acceptable limits.

We would not normally have rejected medication and would never advise anyone to do so without consulting their doctor. However, in this instance the coincidence of Jean Darnall's exceptional sense of assurance about God's healing in answer to prayer, combined with Molly's feeling of improved health, gave us confidence to give up the prescribed tablets. We realised that the drugs might already have had their good effect and that we had no sure evidence that prayer was the direct cause of healing. None the less, the timing was such that we felt encouraged to keep up with our believing prayer about the much more serious problem of Molly's back pain. It also helped us to see that Jean Darnall was a vital factor in God's good plan for us, and the incident gave us a deepened trust in her good sense and in her loving ministry. Later this was to be important.

The reason why we were reluctant to stop taking the prescribed drugs is that Molly and I firmly believe that all healing is God's healing. There are some Christians who imply that it is unbelieving to go to the doctor for healing medicines, and that it is a denial of God's power to heal. Of course, few who hold such views are totally consistent in their behaviour. I have known devout Christians who have laid a great burden on their sick friends by demanding that they should reject prescribed medicines, and simply believe God for healing, who themselves have been wearing spectacles to remedy their imperfect vision!

I have not been so discourteous as to challenge such Christian brothers and sisters directly, but after meeting them, and having heard their strongly held opinions, I have been left feeling that a better view would have been to accept that God, in his love, sometimes uses natural means of healing and sometimes supernatural. Sometimes he works powerfully through scientific medicine, and sometimes he deals directly with our disorders by answering prayer. The skill and wisdom of the wise medical practitioner, with his range of medicines and surgical abilities, is clearly a primary healing gift to mankind. God has always honoured Christian medical work as a tool in winning people to Christ, and his good gifts are never to be despised. Medicines, be they chemicals from herbs or manufactured substances, and the wisdom to apply them for our healing, are generous provisions from God's creation. Surgery, with its marvellous modern skills and complex machinery, is without doubt a gift from our merciful maker. Equally, since there is a long history in the church of miraculous and supernatural healing, in which God moves directly in his creation in answer to believing prayer, we should never allow a limited, scientific approach to the ills of this world to hinder our faith in God's ability to heal our damaged lives.

An approach to healing which accepts both natural and supernatural means of restoring health ties in with the ministry of Jesus himself. As he introduced God's kingdom, the rule of his love in the hearts of men, his priorities were teaching and preaching. His message of the kingdom was constantly confirmed by powerful acts of healing and deliverance:

he went about all Galilee, teaching in their synagogues and preaching the gospel of the kingdom and healing every disease and every infirmity among the people. So his fame spread throughout all Syria, and they brought him all the sick, those afflicted with various diseases and pains, demoniacs, epileptics, and para-lytics, and he healed them. (Matt 4:23–24)

When Jesus dealt with the sick, he did not deny natural remedies. Indeed he often incorporated normal healing practice into his own supernatural healing. In the case of the blind man whose healing is described in Mark 8, Jesus 'spit on his eyes and laid his hands upon him' (v. 23), and as we have already seen Jesus dealt in a similar way with the man who was blind from birth: 'he spat on the ground and made clay of the spittle and anointed the man's eyes with the clay' (John 9:6). He handled the deaf man with an impediment in his speech in a similar way: 'taking him aside from the multitude privately, he put his fingers into his ears, and he spat and touched his tongue; and looking up to heaven, he sighed, and said to him, "Eph-phatha," that is, "Be opened"' (Mark 7:33–34). It was a commonly held belief in the ancient world that spittle had curative qualities, so Jesus was simply taking the methods and customs of his time as part of the healing process. It meant that he did not startle these men with a dramatic encounter of spiritual power. He prepared them gently with his touch.

This combination of the earthly and heavenly dimension of healing, combining the natural medical remedy of the day with believing prayer to God, and an authoritative word of command that the illness should leave, is a pattern for our healing ministry in the church today. A good rule of thumb is always to seek the simple and straightforward remedy first, and only when that fails to look for a miracle.

A friend of mine, who served God as a missionary surgeon in Thailand, tells the story of her own experience of healing when she had cancer diagnosed. It was decided to fly her home to England for further tests and if necessary for surgery. As she journeyed home she was thrilled to discover that on that very day her name was printed in the prayer diary of the missionary society in which she served. Flying high above the clouds, she was conscious of being borne up by the prayers of thousands of Christians all over the world. I asked her why she travelled such a long way for surgery when she might have saved the journey by trusting God for a miracle of healing. It was not that I thought she was wrong in taking such action, since it is exactly what I would have done myself, but I wanted to know how a trained surgeon who had no problem in believing in God's miraculous power would reason things out when she was possibly herself under sentence of death. 'Oh,' she said, 'I reckoned that if God could solve my problem by a bit of simple plumbing, I didn't have to trouble him to provide a miracle.' In fact, when she got to London all the tests were negative. The X-rays did not confirm a previously detected cancer. There was every reason to assume that the healing had been accomplished in answer to prayer. The fact that she made such a long and, in the event, needless journey, only imprinted the episode in her mind with double emphasis of thanksgiving to God for his healing power.

God's people do not always have such a good and balanced view of the natural and supernatural factor in God's provision for them. Quite early on in the Old Testament account of God dealing with Israel in the wilderness, he revealed himself as the God who heals. It happened at a point of difficulty and discouragement in the journeying of the Israelites, when they were tired and thirsty, but found only bitter water to drink. This caused them to express inner bitterness and grumbling against their circumstances, their leader Moses, and their God. They blamed Moses for the trouble, so he turned to God in prayer and God answered with a miracle: 'he cried to the Lord; and the Lord showed him a tree, and he threw it into the water, and the water became sweet' (Exod 15:25). But this sign of kindness and mercy was immediately followed by a very firm command in which God laid down the conditions under which his people could expect healing:

If you will diligently hearken to the voice of the Lord your God, and do that which is right in his eyes, and give heed to his commandments and keep all his statutes, I will put none of the diseases upon you which I put upon the Egyptians; for I am the Lord, your healer. (v. 26)

Healing is therefore fundamental to the character and purpose of God. He wants us whole, and a sure way to miss wholeness is to refuse to go God's way. If only the people of Israel had kept trusting instead of complaining about their tough circumstances, they would have found that help was only just around the next corner. They came to 'twelve springs of water' at Elim (v. 27). Their grumbling caused a needless crisis of prayer and leadership for Moses and a quite unnecessary miracle from God.

Molly and I found this tension between accepting trouble and crying to God for deliverance from her severe back pain a difficult thing to live with. After Jean Darnall's visit to our home, during which the problem of the high blood pressure was dealt with, the back pain became markedly worse. This was really not surprising after five years of constant pain aggravated by giving birth to a bouncing boy who weighed in at 9 lb 4 oz! After only a few months Molly seized up completely and had to be taken into the Royal Orthopaedic Hospital in Birmingham. This was an experience from which we had to learn many lessons about human nature, some good and some bad. Timothy was only four months old at the time, and it was no easy thing to sustain the pattern of busy cathedral ministry, missions outside Birmingham, plus proper care of a young family, with Mum in hospital for several months, fixed rigid on her bed, undergoing traction.

We learnt new lessons about family love, as elderly grandparents dropped everything to help with family needs. We experienced practical help in the home from unexpected sources. Neighbours who had been mere acquaintances before came in to clean and to cook, and through the illness became firm friends. Our GP's wife called in with meals fully prepared and cooked. Others whom we had previously helped came to live in with the family. It was evident that God knew all our needs before we asked and prompted his people to serve and care without us having to ask. That released me for continuing ministry, and because our needs were exactly provided for, it meant that other friends were free to get on with their own work too.

But the troubles were not yet complete. While Molly was stretched out in hospital, Charis was admitted to the Children's Hospital in Birmingham with appendicitis. With two of the family in different hospitals, and entirely dependent on this bevy of Christian friends to keep the home going and the patients visited, I was due to lead a university mission at Hull. It was only at the last minute that I found out that all the other members of the cathedral staff had booked to be away at the same time, and as the junior member I was expected to cover cathedral services on certain days, as well as preaching in Hull.

Such chaos and disorder was ungodly and unacceptable. It seemed to highlight the pattern of attack on our well-being as a family and on our spiritual ministry. As we had come to the conviction that this period of testing could not go on, God gave the same conviction to Jean Darnall, who was one of the assistant missioners at Hull. Satan had overstretched himself this time, because the extremity of our need showed that it was not just a sequence of temptation and illness taking a natural course. The degree of disorder caused us all to come against Satan, the lord of chaos.

As I was about to leave the hospital after visiting Molly, I moved out into the corridor and was amazed to see a figure coming purposefully towards the ward. It was a woman in furs (fitting for an English winter) who seemed to be filling the whole corridor with her presence – sailing along like some stately galleon from the past. It was not at all the time for hospital visitors – indeed I had only gained entrance myself by wearing my dog collar. As the figure approached I recognised the broadly smiling features. It was none other than Jean Darnall! No one could have been more welcome, because by this time we were having to consider surgery in order to deal with the long-term back pain. No medical treatment had provided any relief, nor were any promises given that surgery would solve the problem.

Jean called by as a totally unexpected answer to prayer in our perplexity. It turned out that she had come to Birmingham that evening to appear on a television programme. Having seen from the previous week's mission in Hull how the enemy was totally disrupting our lives and our minstry, Jean had come with renewed faith that this was the time for God's healing and deliverance. She entered the tiny room. It was crowded with beds, although remarkably only two of them were occupied, one by Molly and another by a friend. This was the only evening in weeks when they had been alone and when Jean could exercise personal ministry in privacy. But the reality of prayer was more than the quietness of the night hour and of the small number of people gathered in the ward. There was a divine hush, memorable in its intensity, and that tiny upstairs ward felt to me like some mountain-top chapel in which we were as near to heavenly realities in a physical sense as in terms of spiritual truth and experience.

Firstly Jean prayed with Molly, this time quite confident that after months lying trussed up and immovable in bed, feeding and tidying herself with the help of a driving mirror angled above her head, she would be completely healed of her pain and incapacity. Then she moved to Jane in the next bed, as Molly shared that they had been talking together about the power and love of Jesus Christ. Following X-rays Jane had been told that day that her spine was disintegrating and that she was to be operated on the next morning. Jean prayed for her in the same way and then prophesied that as the surgeons operated they would find a condition quite different from that shown on the X-ray plates and that within not too many days both Molly and Jane would walk out of hospital to go to their homes and families. That prophecy was soon fulfilled for both of them, and Molly's improved health coincided with our call to move from the staff of Birmingham Cathedral as I became vicar of St John's, Harborne, a busy suburb of Birmingham.

But was she completely healed? As we had both prayed for years for this improvement, we could hardly believe that it had actually happened. Charis was also by now out of hospital, and we had no shadow of doubt about the change in her life. Removal of the offending appendix led to a dramatic change in her habits and in her appearance. She started to eat as never before and her body filled out visibly before our eyes. She was no longer a skinny, wasted-looking child. Suddenly she was bonny, bright and energetic. We were grateful to the doctors for skilful diagnosis, treatment and care, but apart from being grateful to God for living in Birmingham with its excellent medical services, I am not sure that we were *full* of thanksgiving to God for all the healing provision that had brought our little one back to health. We rather took it for granted.

With Molly it was different. The healing was plainly due to prayer rather than medical treatment. Or was it? We wondered if, after all, the good effect of weeks of traction had worked, coincidentally, with Jean's prayer ministry. But then there was Jane. When she was operated on, the surgeons did not find the condition that the X-rays led them to expect. Her spine was not in a disintegrated state, and the surgery was a far more simple job than had at first been anticipated. There was measurable improvement which we could certainly attribute to answered prayer. But in Molly's case there was still some pain, and she still had to be very careful. It was very easy to trip over kerbs and to misjudge steps because she had not been walking freely for many months. She still booked in for her manipulation treatment if she jarred her back, but as months went by we had to admit that there was a quite dramatic and life-changing difference.

We hardly dared to assume that at long last our prayers had been unconditionally answered, so we were slow to shout from the roof-tops that a miracle had happened. As we moved to St John's, some five months after leaving hospital, Molly was humping furniture, laying carpets, and painting ceilings, as any housewife would do. What was more, she could lift the children in her arms and cuddle them, as any mother would do. People in the church were urged not to ask too much of her, because 'her health was poor'. It was soon evident that she was as strong as most, and stronger than many. Of course she was still vulnerable. Her body had years of habit to counter as she had moved awkwardly to avoid pain. Wasted muscles had to gain strength, everything was being readjusted as she regained wholeness. But gradually our weak faith was encouraged and we praised God for a lasting transformation and a notable deliverance from pain. God is good, indeed!

More than once we reflected on this. 'Why do you think he took so long to answer our prayers?' Molly would ask. 'I suppose it's partly so that we should know how hopeless our situation seemed to be,' I would reply – not letting on that in my moments of darkest doubt I had had visions of Molly being confined permanently to a wheelchair. 'I'm also sure that there is a sovereignty of God's timing,' I would also add. 'Our prayers are not always answered just when we want, and there are lessons to be learnt from suffering and pain.' 'It's all right for you to speak,' retorted Molly on several occasions, 'it wasn't your back!' But the partnership of suffering is real, in the closeness of family love, and sometimes it is hard for the onlooker who really cares, simply because there is so little that can be done to ease the other's pain.

For a long time we found it hard to understand why

Molly was so fragile and vulnerable, but eventually we decided that most of God's dealings with us are in terms of steady growth and slow progress rather than a crisis act that solves all of life's problems in one go. Conversion is like that. If it is sudden and dramatic, conversion to Christ is usually the culmination of a long time of searching and seeking. It is also only the start of a lifetime of growth into the likeness of Christ. We are never made perfect by God's one-off working in our lives. Why should we demand that healing is always complete after one time of prayer, or one healing service, or one visit of a person with a noted healing gift? It is surely better to think in terms of walking steadily into health. There may be a notable moment of faith and prayer and healing ministry, but after that progress to wholeness is often measured and steady. If we had realised this more clearly we should not have doubted God so often in the first weeks after Jean's prayer, and then our own continued attitude of trust would have been a plus factor in the healing process. As it was, our tendency to doubt was certainly more of a hindrance than a help.

The fact that God does heal in stages is evidenced from the incident at Bethsaida when Jesus restored the sight of a blind man who was brought to him.

> When he had spit on his eyes and laid his hands upon him, he asked him, 'Do you see anything?' And he looked up and said, 'I see men; but they look like trees, walking.' Then again he laid his hands upon his eyes; and he looked intently and was restored, and he saw everything clearly. (Mark 8:23–25)

Commentators have read all sorts of meaning into this healing by stages. Some have said that the partial sight represents the partial revelation given by God to his people in Old Testament times, and that the full vision represents the full revelation of the New Testament given in Jesus. It could just be that as Jesus knew the heart of this man, and the faith of those who brought him, he acted as he did so that they should learn necessary lessons for their own lives – not least to keep trusting Jesus even when healing is not complete.

Many of the difficulties that we have in continuing to believe are due to the unbelieving conditions in which we live. The world around us shouts out its message of secularity and unbelief. Many in the church deem it eccentric to trust God for healing. So we are often in the situation that Jesus found himself in when Mark records 'he could do no mighty work there, except that he laid his hands upon a few sick people and healed them. And he marvelled because of their unbelief' (Mark 6:5–6). This was in his own village, where he was known as 'the carpenter' (v. 3). If our faith is discouraged by unbelief all around us, it is not surprising that we have problems in believing God for healing. In such circumstances the very power of God is limited by human unbelief. At a later stage, when Jesus landed with his disciples at Gennesaret, there was no stopping the flow of healing power as 'the people recognised him' (v. 54). They

> ran about the whole neighbourhood and began to bring sick people on their pallets to any place where they heard he was. And wherever he came, in villages, cities, or country, they laid the sick in the market places, and besought him that they might touch even the fringe of his garment; and as many as touched it were made well. (vv. 55–56)

The very first time that we 'dared' to pray with the laying on of hands during an 'Open to God' session at St John's, some of our most devout and senior Christians walked out of the meeting, unable to cope with a new style of Christian behaviour and a new challenge to Christian faith. Prayer was, in fact, wonderfully answered on that occasion, and our faith was uplifted as we sought to persevere in the healing ministry. This ministry developed notably when a team of elders was established in the congregation. Some two dozen leaders of the church prayed and studied for a whole year before it was agreed that the three ordained priests and three laymen should be recognised as elders who would share various aspects of ministry in the church. At first, this group took a lead in the healing ministry. Nowadays, however, if a person asks for healing prayer at any of our meetings or at Sunday services, the whole congregation will join in prayer, the choir and musicians will worship and praise in a supportive way, and the whole community backs the faith of the elders and others who may minister healing in Christ's name. There is a tremendous sense of mutual backing, support and encouragement, and the long, drawn-out experience of healing that Molly and I were called to go through can bear its fruit in the ongoing instruction and help we can give to those who are themselves walking into health.

15   Deliver us from evil

A short time after her healing experience, Molly staggered through the glass doors of the Carrs Lane Church Centre in Birmingham, clutching her head. She almost fell into my arms as I returned to the building following a lively Christian meeting of praise, worship, gospel preaching and healing.

'My head, my head,' she cried, 'It's as though somebody hit me hard on the head with a hammer, just at the top of the stairs over there.'

I looked across the crowded vestibule and could see nothing but groups of Christians, excited by the meetings, talking animatedly before the church doors were finally closed. Then the facts emerged. Molly had just been talking to a woman named Joy at the top of a long flight of stone stairs. Both had quite recently experienced a remarkable healing and deliverance, in which drug and hospital treatment and direct prayer ministry had combined to bring peace to their lives. Molly had come to know healing from years of pain in her back (see chapter fourteen) and Joy had found deliverance from severe satanic attack. Christians were glad because of their healing, angels were rejoicing, God's name was praised, and the enemy of souls was disquieted. Somehow he produced the effect of a hammer blow on the top of Molly's head, so that she was nearly sent hurtling down the long flight of stone stairs, just as her back was recovering from years of pain and serious injury. Or did one of the people crowding around her suddenly produce a weapon hidden in a raincoat pocket? Did she imagine it? Or was it some chastening blow from God himself? The possible explanations seemed ludicrous and blasphemous. This must be part of the battle. The enemy was at work in a way which defied rational explanation.

Only the previous Saturday I had heard from Joy for the very first time. Her telephone call came soon after an early morning prayer time at church during which all the warning signs of spiritual danger ahead rang, flashed and buzzed at one and the same time. Sitting on a hard chair at an early morning hour was in itself an occupation burdensome to the flesh, but then to feel goose pimples of fear seemed to add spiritual insult to the physical injury. The red warning light shone when one of my senior lay readers prayed a fervent prayer for protection for me as I was to make a journey later that day in connection with a weekend of preaching ministry at the University of Southampton and in the local churches. The sense of threat against me was renewed when the telephone rang and Joy came on the line with her cry for help. Something in her voice stimulated a renewed sense of fear, and it seemed as though I was being warned of danger ahead as surely as Paul was warned by the prophet Agabus that if he journeyed to Jerusalem he would risk danger and imprisonment (Acts 21:10–11). The warning was given in order that I should take special care. I had no intention of giving up the journey altogether.

The first threat of danger came halfway along the Warwick by-pass. Driving at around seventy miles an hour in the outside lane of a dual carriageway, with traffic bunched all around, there was a sudden blow-out of my rear off-side tyre. The car snaked, I prayed, and all the other cars disappeared mysteriously from the scene. Refusing to panic, I pulled across to the hard shoulder and stopped the car in order to investigate the cause of the unexpected emergency. It was just a nail in a brand new tyre, but it might have been a nail hammered into a coffin without the protecting mercy of God.

The second point of danger that weekend came when praying with a research student at the university. As a child he had committed his life to Satan, and after a struggle he had given his life to Christ during a mission at Southampton University in which I had shared some years before. After years of mental and spiritual disorder he came to a crisis of deliverance on the Sunday afternoon of this weekend's visit. As I prayed with him in his room he became positively violent as he writhed and struggled on the floor before coming to a new freedom and healing in Christ.

I drove home from that weekend with special care and vigilance. Too many times in the past there had been an extraordinary coincidence of punctures and accidents at a time of spiritual conflict and blessing. Much contemporary literature warns of the close link between the prayer wish of people committed to evil and various accidents suffered by Christian workers. In his book *The Experiences of a Present Day Exorcist* (Kimber, 1970), Father Donald Oman tells of how he was involved with an institute of scientific research in investigations into inexplicable road accidents. It was discovered in one instance that when two drivers recovered from a head-on accident, both claimed a sudden, irresistible urge to drive a collision course which took them uncontrollably into each other's path. A girl committed to witchcraft once told me how she had sent her fiancé away without her blessing, and that he had, not surprisingly to her, had a serious collision on his way home, and at that point in time was suffering in hospital from irreversible brain damage. He died a fortnight later. No wonder I prayed especially for God to 'preserve my going out and my coming in' on the journey home from that particular weekend of ministry.

Two days later, Joy came. A teacher and a Christian, she was smartly dressed, her brown hair tied back and fastened with a new bow, and at first sight she was just another girl in a crowd. There was no particular evidence of internal turmoil, no apparent sign of nervousness, no hint of inner conflict. Yet her telephone call had been a desperate cry for help. Only afterwards did she confess that her mental image of me, a complete stranger, had been that of a little old man with scores of years of experience in Christian ministry! Little did she know that here was someone just beginning to find the answer to Satan's tactics, and learning in the school of daily experience how he wants to disturb God's purpose and destroy human freedom.

Her problem was epilepsy. At least that is what some doctors had called it, though having been to a leading London specialist there was some confusion over the diagnosis. That was the first starred point in my notes – 'confusion of diagnosis'. Again and again in mental or physical illness, where there is a confusion of expert scientific opinion, the spiritual counsellor may find that at the back of an apparent disorder of body or mind there may be a complicating spiritual factor. Physicians who have no spiritual dimension at all in their understanding of human dis-ease have taught us for years how important the interaction of mind and body is. What a shame it is that because not all believe that man is meant to live at the level of body, mind and spirit, spiritual disorders are often ignored.

The story came out. All the trouble seemed to start with a family row. Joy stopped living with her sister and went to find her own digs. She showed a remarkable vehemence in describing her new landlord. 'If ever there was a man demon possessed, it was him!' Here was the second starred entry in my notes – 'demon possessed'. A most unusual term for somebody from Joy's particular background, and certainly not a phrase that I would have brought into the conversation. The next extraordinary juxtaposition of events was that just after she moved in with this 'evil' man, Joy also suffered serious injury in a car accident when she was knocked down

118

on a pedestrian crossing. It was from that time that her suspected epileptic trouble started, and the coincidence of these events led to another starred entry in the notes.

During a period of breakdown of health, both mental and physical, other unpleasant events occurred. One vivid memory was of an evening following a heavy day of teaching at school, when resting on the couch in her flat she heard footsteps coming up the staircase. Through the partly open door she saw a black shape go past the door and into the bathroom, where the taps were turned on and she heard the sound of running water. After a time, when the sound of water did not stop, she went to investigate, despite the chill of fear that came over her, but there was no one to be seen in the bathroom. She never did succeed in tracing any human visitor to the flat that evening. Here was another starred entry for the case notes.

The time for prayer had come. I explained to Joy how all these happenings had crowded like a pile of unwanted rubbish into her experience, and all needed to be swept away as God came in by his Spirit to do a spring-clean in these untidy and disordered areas of her life. There was the guilt about a broken relationship with her sister, which needed God's forgiveness; there was the fear of her landlord, which needed the perfect love of God's Holy Spirit to cast it out; there was the physical hurt from the car accident, with the continuing pattern of epilepsy, that needed God's touch of healing; there was the mental strain and pain, which needed the peace which Jesus offered to those who put their trust in him. No wonder she was tempted to despair with so many points of weakness which Satan could use for his attack. Just as he tempted Jesus in the wilderness at his points of tiredness and loneliness and hunger and insecurity about the future, so he tempted Joy at the points of weakness and damage in her life. I felt a sense of surging anger against the evil one as I looked at my notes and saw a story of intrusion and invasion into a previously happy Christian life.

But one thing troubled me. I always found that people held like this in the enemy's grip only came to healing and deliverance when I prayed in tongues in a particular way that had become an inevitable part of this prayer ministry to needy people. When Paul in Ephesians 6 outlines the special armour that God gives to Christians in fighting against the powerful evil forces at the disposal of the devil, he ends up with two weapons to be used for attack against the power of the enemy. One of these is the 'sword of the Spirit, which is the word of God' (v. 17), and the other is prayer 'in the Spirit' (v. 18). 'Pray at all times in the Spirit,' says Paul, 'with all prayer and supplication.' I would have to pray in a Spirit-given language with Joy.

Joy would be used to me quoting the Bible, I reasoned, since that would be a common thing in her Christian background, but what about praying in tongues? Yet I knew that in my particular pattern of ministry this gift which had been given some time previously was the key factor in bringing a person out of the power of Satan and under the rule of Jesus Christ. When I had prayed without using the gift in times past, people had not been helped. When I gave up my own fear and embarrassment, and used the gift God's Spirit had given, there was often healing and deliverance. There was nothing for it, I had to explain to Joy the gift and the need to use it and then get on with the job.

Joy told me afterwards how she felt during the time of prayer. The crunch came when we prayed against the influence of her landlord. As I resisted the devil and commanded him and his agents back to the place where they belong under the authority of Christ, and then prayed with the laying on of hands for the love of God to come with healing fullness into the vacated part of her experience, she wanted inside herself to cry out, 'He's evil, he's evil, he's evil!' Joy was discerning the evil influence of her landlord on her life. She felt as though she was lifted physically to the ceiling, forcing against the gentle pressure of my hands. Then after a continuing time of fight and struggle she slumped at peace in her chair.

In the follow-up discussion, we talked very fully about how God's deliverance from evil bondage can be experienced in a moment of time, but also how the growth into wholeness is a steady and progressive thing. The principle of progressive growth and development is built into the whole of God's created world, and so much heartache is caused to Christian people who assume that one decisive act of God's intervention means that all the fighting, and all the struggle, and all the disorder, is forever finished. The picture I used was of a chaotically untidy attic. Furniture, books, magazines and discarded articles of all sorts are jumbled together in a mountain of disturbance. If one article is moved, the whole heap erupts into a slithering mass, uncontrollable and uncontrolled. But with perseverance the determined spring-cleaner manages to open the door a few inches, and begins to bring the troubled mess out into the open. Eventually some of the cluttered objects are removed, but even when the offensive items are taken right away and the door can open wide, it is evident that the clearing-up process will take much longer than was at first expected.

So it is with many lives. Painful memories, past mistakes, misunderstandings, fears, regrets and rejections are all stored away, hopefully forgotten in the attic of our past experience. We shut the door, and live for a long time glad that we can't open it more than an inch or two now and again. And yet the pain and untidiness is there.

Sometimes it seems as though the pains go back to the discomfort of the womb or the pain of birth. An unwanted baby, conceived out of love or wedlock, picks up the impressions of fear and rejection, of insecurity and perhaps even of hatred in the mother's experience. Sometimes because of some illness, the new-born life is snatched away from its mother's love into the clinical safety of a heartless incubator. Sometimes the child is born into a tug-of-love situation, or even the cool respectability of a 'Christian' home, where love is a word in the Bible dictionary rather than an experience in the heart. Sometimes the little life is looked to as a source of affection and love because there is no love left between mother and father, and instead of love being poured into the baby's experience a parent unwittingly drains its last resource and sucks out its last ability to love. Sometimes the pain comes later with a sense of competition with other brothers and sisters, or with a demand to come up to some standard of perfection or success in some area of human attainment. How often the well-meaning academic, or ambitious musician, or the hopeful sporting parent presses a child to a sense of unredeemable failure by their excessive demand. This creates at the worst a sense of self-hatred and at the best a feeling of personal unworthiness.

Joy's problems did not go back that far, but the enemy made sure he found an opportunity to fill her life with torment and fear. But as God's broom swept clean, the sort-out was only just beginning – for her and for us. I returned home from that time of prayer to find Molly locked in pain, despite a special prayer of protection for her. It seemed that the enemy's comeback in the battle was always to choose her weakest point, and shake our faith in God's victory. Sharing our concern with other Christians, it was a comfort to find that often there was a similar pattern of comeback on others engaged in such work for Christ, and we were comforted by their fellow-sufferings. The pain in the back at the time of ministering to Joy, the blow on the head days later on meeting her in the city-centre, the fear, the doubt, the embarrassment, the searching after wisdom and skill in ministry – all were part of a learning process in fighting the powers of darkness and learning to minister in Jesus' name.

Today, through the remarkable ministry of John

Wimber and his team from the Vineyard Fellowship in the United States, God's church is being reminded of the authority it has in Jesus' name over all the power of the evil one. Their ministry focuses in a dramatic way what God has been doing on a smaller scale in myriads of churches all over the world during the last twenty-five years. The story of Joy is just one example of hundreds that could be told from our parish alone. How do we explain this phenomenon?

Primarily it is to do with the weakness and decline of the church. Although I have always been fortunate to minister in situations of church growth, I have been painfully aware that Christians represent only a tiny minority of the total population of the UK. As a missionary society in a secular state, British Christians have had to cry to God for help. A new Spirit of prayer has caused many Christians to claim God's power as the disciples of Jesus did at Pentecost. Jesus promised power, so they claimed it, for they were only a tiny handful committed to win the whole of the world for Christ.

16   Welcome death

'Please, please, come quickly. We think the old boy's gone, and his eyes won't shut!' It was an early morning call from the daughter of a family who lived next door to us. We had not lived all that long in Birmingham, having recently begun our work at the cathedral there. Our contact with our next door neighbours was friendly, but casual rather than close. The request was therefore a surprise, to say the least. It is one thing to do all the professional things that a clergyman has to do to help bereaved relatives and deal with funeral services at the cemetery or crematorium. It is quite another thing to deal with the corpse!

Of course, this was not always the case. Before the days of clinical efficiency which takes death out of the home and into the mortuary or the undertaker's chapel of rest, it was very common for the clergyman to be asked for such practical help. Along with others who have a caring role in the community, he would be expected to lay out a body as well as to comfort grieving relatives. I was fortunate enough to be taught this art in the course of lectures on pastoral care at Oak Hill, where I trained for the ministry. The training stood me in good stead as I hurried next door to see if 'the old boy' had really died or not.

As we gathered around his bedside in a downstairs room, it was evident that there was not a breath of life left in his body. He was warm, but totally still and motionless, and with his eyes wide open and rolled back in his head, he presented an awesome sight. My college training had insisted on the use of two old-style copper pennies to hold the eyelids down, but decimalisation had just been introduced, so pennies were no longer available. I fished in my pocket and found two 10p pieces, reflecting as I used them that not only had the cost of living risen, but the cost of dying had also suddenly jumped. As I stayed and prayed with the man's widow and her daughter, the eyelids settled and the dead body presented a picture of sleep and of peace. The intense gratitude of the two women seemed out of all proportion to the small service rendered, but most important of all, the door had been opened for sharing more of Christ's gospel at a later time.

When I got home Molly was amazed that I had coped with the experience so well. She is usually the practical one in the partnership and would expect to be able to shut 'the old boy's eyes' and indeed to lay him out completely without the help of any college lectures on the subject. What she also knew was that it was only through becoming a Christian that I had been able to overcome a deep-rooted fear of death. At the human level this went back to childhood experiences. I remember being terrified of entering the room in which my grandmother had been laid out in her coffin at her home in Sussex. There seemed to be a family conspiracy not to tell me why her body was there, or what happens when a person dies. The Victorian tradition of our family was that six year old boys should be seen and not heard, so it was out of the question (or so it seemed) to ask about my inner fears. At the spiritual level, though I did not realise it at the time, it is Satan's tactic to hold us in fear of death. Hebrews 2:14 says that Jesus himself partook of our nature 'that through death he might destroy him who has the power of death, that is, the devil, and deliver all those who through fear of death were subject to lifelong bondage'.

It is this grip of fear that leads to so many irrational actions when a loved one is dying. Nowadays, when so many doctors are open and honest about terminal illness and keep both patient and family as informed as they can about life expectancy, the knowledge of imminent death has to be faced by many people. And yet so few take the prospect of death in their stride. I remember when our bishop, Dr Hugh Montefiore, was staying with us over a long weekend, as our turn had come for a parish visitation, he spoke at morning assembly in our local secondary school and then faced a barrage of questions from a group of fourth-form girls. One of them asked him outright, 'Are you afraid of death?' The bishop thought for a moment and said, 'No, honestly, I'm not afraid of death, but I'm afraid of dying.' If we're honest, many of us would echo that statement. Those of us who have seen a loved one dying from a cruel cancer know just what Paul meant when he spoke of death as our 'last enemy' (1 Cor 15:26). But it's the process of dying which is so fearful, not necessarily death itself. All of us are grateful for the honest account that David Watson has given in his last book *Fear No Evil* (Hodder & Stoughton 1984) as he vividly portrays the progression from that clutch of fear when cancer was first announced to the sense of acceptance that death was near. He writes:

As I lay there in the early hours of the morning [facing death], I knew that I had to trust someone about the future; and there is no-one in the history of the world that I would rather trust than Jesus Christ . . . I knew my Christianity was not built on a dream, a religious idea or a fictional character. It was solidly based on a historical person. (p. 44–45)

My own brushes with the spectre of death have given me quite a new perspective about dying and have positively encouraged my faith in God's good dealings with his people when they die. As a young Christian I was aware of Bible promises, and my trust in what the New Testament said about death and dying largely removed the irrational childhood fear that had held me in bondage for so long. I was particularly impressed by the attitude of Stephen, the first Christian martyr, who when he was stoned to death, with an angry crowd grinding their teeth against him

> full of the Holy Spirit, gazed into heaven and saw the glory of God, and Jesus standing at the right hand of God . . . And as they were stoning Stephen, he prayed, 'Lord Jesus, receive my spirit.' And he knelt down and cried with a loud voice, 'Lord, do not hold this sin against them.' And when he had said this, he fell asleep. (Acts 7:55–60)

My head said, 'Lord, if that is what it's like, there is no problem. You obviously give very special help to a person when they are dying, especially when they die directly in the gospel cause.'

In addition to the account of Stephen's death, I was also struck by Paul's confidence when he wrote to the Christians at Philippi:

> For me to live is Christ, and to die is gain. If it is to be life in the flesh, that means fruitful labour for me. Yet which I shall choose I cannot tell. I am hard pressed between the two. My desire is to depart and be with Christ, for that is far better. But to remain in the flesh is more necessary on your account. (Phil 1:21–24)

My head said: 'Lord, I must have that view of life and death if the resurrection of Jesus is true. It must be better "to depart and be with Christ", but honestly, though I can say it with my mind, I am not sure if my heart is really there yet.'

My attitudes were first put to the test during a long spell in hospital in 1972. My illness mystified the doctors for weeks, as test after test proved negative. When surgery was proposed, the illness was still not diagnosed, and Molly was warned by one of the medical team

that the operation might reveal a serious condition. I was
not told how critical the situation was, but after several
months of feeling seriously unwell I was at a low point
physically, mentally and spiritually – a prime opportunity for satanic attack. On the night before the operation,
thoughts of death loomed large. It could have been due to
natural panic and fear, though I was not afraid of
surgery. I was actually looking forward to some action –
any action after weeks and months of indecision. I believe rather that the crisis of doubt was typical of that
which many Christians experience during a time in hospital. I first met it with an elderly and extremely godly
missionary to deep sea fishermen. He had worked all his
life sharing his glad faith with some of the toughest men
in the seafaring community. And yet in hospital, facing
what proved to be a terminal illness, he crumpled into
doubt and fear. He lost confidence that God had forgiven
all his sins. He wondered after years in the Methodist
ministry whether he was a Christian at all.

A similar thing happened to a former church member,
one of the godliest men I have ever known, a former
church warden of St John's Harborne. He went into
hospital and found it a devastating time of spiritual
testing. Night and day Satan attacked him, so that
although he had always been a man of superbly strong
faith who communed with his Lord in prayer for hours
every day, he could no longer pray at all. He became
weak and despairing until, praying strongly in Jesus'
name, we commanded the enemy away from him. The
transformation and relief this afforded was marked. He
was restored to his customary attitude of buoyant faith
and bold witness, and became his normal outgoing,
caring self. During his time of affliction and temptation
he had been preoccupied with himself and his own
needs. Now he had found a renewed concern for staff
and other patients, and in his very gracious way shared
his faith in Jesus Christ with them.

It should be obvious to any Christian that the devil is

likely to choose such a time to attack, but I confess that it was a long time before I presumed to pray definitely for such deliverance from satanic testing of those in hospital – and notably for people whom I would have expected to show really strong faith in Christ in adverse circumstances. It is the enemy's opportune time because the patient is likely in any case to be feeling low through illness. He is alone, cut off from home and family. He is facing the unknown as far as ward routine, hospital habits and customs, and eventual treatment or diagnosis are concerned. It is also often difficult to sleep in hospital because of noise and disturbance and because after a long time of relative inactivity through illness, little sleep is required. The enemy of souls always works overtime in the dark hours, when we feel especially alone and cut off from human companionship.

My own hospital crisis came one night. The ward was unusually quiet. No one was clattering trolleys or rushing emergency equipment to a bedside. Patients were mostly snoring gently or stirring in troubled sleep. The only nurse in evidence was reading quietly by a shaded lamp at a table near the centre of the ward. But I was wide awake. Sleep was a million miles away, and thoughts of what lay ahead predominated. 'What will they find when they open up? Why did Molly look so worried when she left this evening? What have they told her that they haven't told me? Why are they just opening up to investigate, when we were led to pray at church that they would make a clear diagnosis before surgery was required? Supposing they find a growth? Supposing the growth is malignant? Why did my body shake all over in a quite uncontrollable way yesterday, differently from anything else I have experienced previously? Why does no one understand how really ill I feel? I am sure I cannot survive much longer like this!'

It was the 'poor me' syndrome. It was self, self, self. I was bothered about me and my future, more than for Molly and the children, let alone than for God and his purpose. But it is supremely when we are self-concerned that Satan finds his opportunity. It was just like that for Jesus. He was tempted in the wilderness when he was alone and hungry, and it was the easiest thing in the world for Satan to suggest that Jesus should meet his inner hunger by turning stones into bread. And if the enemy could dare to try it on with the Master, he will certainly try it on with us, his stumbling disciples. That night he tried it on with me. For a while it was struggle and conflict, argument and counter argument.

To begin with it's not always clear at such a time whether a serious attack of Satan is under way or whether you are just feeling negative and depressed in spirit. If there was a manifestation of evil in the room by some horrible visual image or a sense of unusually severe coldness, it would be an instinctive response to cry out to God for help and to resist Satan, using Scripture verses, just as Jesus did in his time of temptation. However, when the testing is at the level of our thought processes, it is much harder to discern whether or not we are in for a heavy battering from the enemy. The safest thing to do as soon as black images fill our minds, along with accusing thoughts and doubts about the truth of God's good promises to us, is to pray firmly against Satan's working in our hearts, resisting him 'firm in our faith' (cf. 1 Pet 5:9). Of course, we must not become preoccupied with the devil and his power, but it is very much safer to counterattack strongly before his subtle and evil suggestions and fears fill our minds. Once he dominates our thinking it is much harder to fight back against him.

No wonder the New Testament is full of many images of warfare. No wonder there are so many battle hymns for Christians to sing. The Christian life is a constant fight against the evil one. In Ephesians 6, having listed our duties in the church, in marriage and family life, and in the world of work, Paul concludes with a vivid description of spiritual warfare. Our battle with Satan is as real as all our everyday duties of relationship in the church and in the world, and for it we need to 'put on the whole armour of God' (Eph 6:11). Paul lists all the parts of the armour – and they represent qualities of the new life of Christ given to us by God's Holy Spirit: 'gird your loins with truth; put on the breastplate of righteousness; put the equipment of the gospel of peace on your feet; take the shield of faith, the helmet of salvation, and the sword of the Spirit, which is the word of God, and finally pray at all times in the Spirit' (cf. Eph 6:14–18).

Some Christians find it helpful to visualise themselves putting on each item of armour every day, in order to be ready to counter Satan's attack. It is certainly vital to seize hold of all our weapons, both for defence and attack, when the battle begins. Of ourselves, we are no match at all for 'the wiles of the devil' (v. 11). It is always an unequal struggle because 'we are not contending against flesh and blood, but against the principalities, against the powers, against the world rulers of this present darkness, against the spiritual hosts of wickedness in the heavenly places' (v. 12). This is why we need 'the whole armour of God' (v. 11) even to stand against Satan. And that is our call – 'to stand against the wiles of the devil' (v. 11); to 'withstand in the evil day, and having done all, to stand' (v. 13). We are to stand our ground while we are under assault, not to gain ground or to lose ground.

In my childhood I used to stay at my uncle's farm in Sussex during the long weeks of summer. It was a small dairy farm where milk was produced, processed and delivered from the churn by horse and cart to the customer's door. I was taught to milk by hand on Elsie, a brown and white Jersey cow with a conveniently paralysed right near leg. It could neither kick the milk bucket over nor knock me off my three-legged stool if it took offence at my amateurish technique. But my favourite bovine companion was Bill the bull. He was a huge brown and white Herefordshire bull with splendid horizontal horns and a shining ring in his nose. I reckoned that we had a good relationship going and that he was genuinely my friend. Certainly, tethered up in his stall he only grunted kindly at me, and never showed a moment's violence or antagonism. 'Watch him,' the cowhand would say, 'you never know with a bull. Never trust him out in the field, and never get in a corner with him in the cow-shed. He'll go for yer.'

I remembered that advice when I was sauntering through the field at the back of the farm. The cows were grazing peacefully, and some distance away I could see Bill eyeing me as I passed through the herd. Whether my red shirt caught his eye, or whether he was in a bad mood that morning I do not know, but suddenly he was trotting menacingly towards me. I walked faster, but did not want to give him any impression of fright or panic. Soon his head was down and he was coming for me at full gallop. I headed for the nearest gate as hard as I could, but within seconds it was obvious that I had no chance of getting to the gate before he had me on his horns. As I ran I saw a stick on the ground, or rather, it was more of a reed than a stick. It was certainly not an adequate weapon against Bill in full flight. But remembering all the advice I had ever heard about man's mastery over animals, I picked the reed up and stood my ground, staring him firmly in the eye. Snorting hard, Bill stopped and stared back at me. Threatening him fiercely with the bent reed, I drew myself up to my full height of 4 ft 9 in, and as Bill turned his head away, I then backed slowly to the gate. It was an adventure and a half for a nine year old, but it taught a lesson of immense significance in spiritual warfare. If you cannot win by brute strength or by hasty retreat, stand your ground. Your weapons may seem inadequate, but because they are God-given they enable you to win in the warfare against Satan.

I had to remember that during the night of conflict in hospital. Instead of being pushed back into doubt, despair and a fear of death, I had to take a stand against the evil one. 'Get away Satan, in Jesus' name! I resist you firm in my faith. The Bible says "Resist the devil and he will flee from you." Jesus in me is stronger than you in the world. Jesus is stronger than the strongest man around.' I hurled these and other Bible verses at the enemy, and claimed God's presence with me by his Holy Spirit. Primarily I focused on all that Jesus had won for me on the cross and by the power of his resurrection: 'Thank you Jesus that when you died on the cross it was not only to forgive my sins, but it was to rob Satan of his power so that death could not hold you, but on the third day you were raised up by God's power. Thank you Jesus that you are alive today and are with me and in me by God's Spirit.'

And as I prayed positive words, claiming the truth of God in place of Satan's lies, and the victory of God over all the power of the evil one, the whole of my surroundings seem to change. I was no longer conscious of the dimly lit ward and the hospital smells. It was as though I was high up on a mountain, worshipping God in a quiet sanctuary. The shaded light above my bed seemed to be transformed so that there was a translucent quality about the scene. There, for hours, I was carried with praise into the presence of God. The fight with Satan was over. He had left – a defeated foe. The presence of God was real – supremely real. And the peace of God did 'pass all understanding' (cf. Phil 4:7).

Any thoughts of a dark future were now transformed by God's bright presence. At that point my confidence was not just in promises and texts from the Bible which were in my head. It is vital to be trusting God's word, but it is not easy to claim promises when Satan is sowing doubts. Now the assurance of God's presence and protection was a reality of heart experience as well as of head knowledge.

Someone may query whether it is right to emphasise a mystical experience to such a degree, since we are called to 'walk by faith, not by sight' (2 Cor 5:7). I can only say that I was not seeking a special 'experience'. I was fighting Satan at the time. The glorious awareness of the brightness and glory of the living God was an unexpected and gracious bonus, just like the time when Jesus was transfigured before Peter, James and John. Jesus 'led them up a high mountain apart by themselves; and he was transfigured before them, and his garments became glistening, intensely white, as no fuller on earth could bleach them' (Mark 9:2–3). We cannot deny them their special experience of the glory of Jesus. They could not live with that brightness of glory all the time, though Peter for one wanted to set up tent and stay on the mountain top. But though they had to leave behind the high experience of Jesus on the mountain, it was an experience that never left them (2 Pet 1:17–18), and was part of the revelation of God to their lives.

That's how it was for me. On the one hand the experience confirmed the promise that there is always a way of escape from satanic temptation. Paul reminds us that 'No temptation has overtaken you that is not common to man. God is faithful, and he will not let you be tempted beyond your strength, but with the temptation will also provide the way of escape, that you may be able to endure it' (1 Cor 10:13). In this instance, *the* way of escape for me was to be lifted up into an unforgettable sense of the majesty and the presence of God. Although I was in the dark about my illness and was unsure what the future held, after that night one thing was certain – God is good and glorious, and I could as ever trust everything to him. Doubt was unthinkable in the light of this new revelation of love. Such an experience did not make the promises of the Bible any more true, it did, however, bring them alive to me in a new way.

I knew very little about the next morning because I was early on the list for surgery. My biggest thrill was when the registrar called by and said that they were no longer to perform an investigative operation. The team had decided to do an appendectomy because they were at last sure that it was an appendix problem. This diagnosis – in the nick of time – was what I had been longing for, because the only thing that had become clear in prayer with the elders of St John's was that we should ask God to give the hospital doctors a very clear ability to diagnose exactly what was wrong. It had puzzled me throughout the weeks in hospital that this diagnosis had not been achieved sooner. In the event the offending organ, together with a number of lesions and a lump of fat that had formed protectively round it, was removed.

'You've had a burst appendix, you know,' the registrar told me, when he called after the operation was over. 'When did that happen? You must have known about it,' he said. 'I've not a clue,' I replied in all honesty, 'but I'll ask Molly if she can recall when it might have happened.' I was totally mystified by the suggestion that there had been a previous crisis of which I could hardly be unaware, so I quizzed Molly as soon as she came to visit me. 'Oh,' she replied, 'it must have been that time on holiday in Scotland when you disappeared for two hours.' 'When I what?' I asked, amazed. She reminded me of one afternoon on the beach when I had left the family to find the nearest toilets. They were some distance from the promenade at Girvan, and on the way back I recalled having excruciating abdominal pain. I had to lie down on some grass beside the promenade, and must have lain there like a dead thing for nearly two hours. When I came round I went straight back to the family, assuming I had been absent for only ten minutes with what I took to be stomach ache. I wondered at their slight sense of panic and fuss, but had no idea that I had been missing for two hours.

The mystery solved, I could only be doubly grateful for surviving both the burst appendix and the surgery three years later. Perhaps most of all I was grateful that the extremity of illness led to a new manifestation of God's love, so that in one sense because of illness there was a new ability to trust the Lord regardless of suffering or any dark thoughts of death. Those who demand instant healing from God for all occasions of illness fail to see the wider purposes of God's love. They do not allow the sick person to learn the lessons of trust and fresh discovery that the experience of illness can bring. They fail to see that even affliction can be creative – and to miss that is to miss the meaning of the cross. The death of Jesus was entirely voluntary. He said that no man could take his life from him: 'I lay it down of my own accord' (John 10:18). He had to suffer and die if the world was to be rescued. Peter expressed the paradox of the cross in his very first post-Pentecost sermon: 'this Jesus, delivered up according to the definite plan and foreknowledge of God, you crucified and killed by the hands of lawless men' (Acts 2:23). It was 'for the joy that was set before him' that Jesus 'endured the cross, despising the shame, and is seated at the right hand of the throne of God' (Heb 12:2).

Some people are made bitter by their sufferings, but I have known many Christians who have looked back on a time of testing with gratitude. When everything in life seemed to be getting worse and worse, and when death seemed the only way out, having survived the time of trial they were as grateful for the pain as for the deliverance from it.

Despite all that happened through this particular breakdown in health, I still wondered in subsequent years just what it was like to be even closer to death than that experience allowed. A number of people in our congregation have related stories of 'coming back' from the dead, and have encouraged me in their descriptions of a very positive anticipation of the afterlife.

One was George, who had taught mathematics in the university of Addis Ababa, and found his call to the Anglican ministry through a vision of God which was given to him during an extended time when his heart had stopped beating following a heart attack. He saw something of the glory of heaven, and its joy, and Christ on a white horse, but the message that came to him plainly was that he had more work to do for God on earth, and though he could be glad at receiving a foretaste of heaven, it was not for him yet.

Another was Harry, whom I visited just fifteen minutes before he died. Harry lived locally in Harborne and was born of exceedingly godly parents, but had fallen right away from the church. His mother had prayed for him earnestly to the end, and he was getting back into touch with Christian people. When I met him in hospital he was in the seventh heaven! His face radiated the beauty of Christ and he could not stop pouring out graphic details of his vision of heaven which came while doctors worked on him during a seizure which had occurred only a short time before. He promised that if he survived, life would never be the same again, and his words were full of vows of repentance for past sin and a willingness to trust in Jesus and his forgiveness for the rest of his days. He needed time and opportunity to prove his point, and this he never had, but for me the incident was so real that although Harry could not prove his repentance and faith in a changed lifestyle, his whole being was clear testimony to God's intervening mercy and grace.

I had to wait until 1985 for a similar close encounter with death. Because the experience was not this time linked with a long-term illness, I was amazed to discover that it could be a really creative and pleasurable happening.

The crisis came right at the start of a funeral service in the local crematorium. As I began to walk ahead of the coffin, speaking Jesus' own strong words of assurance: 'I am the resurrection and the life; he who believes in me, though he die, yet shall he live, and whoever lives and believes in me shall never die' (John 11:25), I was aware that all was not well. Waves of giddiness came over me and I was clutching for breath. I just about survived the twenty-third Psalm, but could give the people none of the normal words of Christian hope, challenge and expectancy. I wanted to share that as Christ is 'the first' fruits of those who have fallen asleep' (1 Cor 15:20), so we can follow him into the sleep of death and the resurrection to new life as we turn to him and trust him. That we need no more fear death, if we are Christians, than we fear falling asleep most nights of our lives. That the Bible promises that as we all fall asleep in physical death, so we shall all wake up to a new day – some of us sadly to the day of judgment, if we choose to live without God – but some of us, if we 'belong to Christ' (1 Cor 15:23), will wake up to meet him when he comes again to this world to rule and to reign, 'For he must reign until he has put all his enemies under his feet. The last enemy to be destroyed is death' (vv. 25–26).

These and other words would have been said, but I could only apologise for being unwell, as I brought the service to a premature close. To this day I do not know whether or not the coffin was lowered. However, I was certainly laid out and laid low, with waves of unconsciousness that overtook me with ever-increasing intensity and with a sort of breathlessness that threatened to take me out of the crematorium vestry and into eternity. 'This is funny,' I thought, 'I think I'm dying. It's not at all how I imagined it would be. Lord you are so good, and I certainly want to meet you. Lord, why am I not more concerned for Molly and the family? Isn't that rather selfish of me – to be glad to go, not the least bit worried for their sake? But I know you will take care of them and be with them.'

I knew that Alf, the attendant of the crematorium, had made necessary phone calls to the vicarage and the church. I felt that survival time was limited. Eventually my colleague Bill Merrington arrived with Edi my secretary in hot pursuit, and between them they called an ambulance.

Two and a half hours went, I know not where. I remember questions being flung at me in the ambulance: 'What's your name, mate? Where do you live?' But I had no strength to answer properly. I remember the nurse in the emergency admissions unit at the hospital grumbling and groaning because it was time to go off duty, and here was another body on a stretcher. I felt so in the way. 'Why don't I just go, Lord?'

But after the nursing staff took several attempts to rig up wires and rubber suckers to get the right bleeps on the complex machinery, Molly was allowed into the cubicle and somehow from that moment I know that Paul's words which had always meant so much to me were vivid and real for this situation: 'My desire is to depart and be with Christ, for that is far better. But to remain in the flesh is more necessary on your account' (Phil 1:23–24).

In retrospect, it was a good experience. It was good to know that faith in the victory and resurrection of Jesus Christ does work when you think you are dying. His forgiveness is so complete that there is no need to go over a checklist of favourite sins to get yourself sorted out before meeting God. That is part of everyday Christian experience, and we must be up-to-date in repenting and believing for forgiveness, so that we are ready to die at any moment. It was good to have the confidence that loved ones left behind are in God's safe hands. It was also exceedingly important for me that I did not have a special mystical experience like George or Harry, or even like that one years before in the hospital ward. It was an extremely matter-of-fact, enjoyable and practical time of straight dealing with the Lord in his goodness.

Of course the reason why all fear of death in such circumstances is taken away, together with our normal human sense of guilt and failure, is because of all that Jesus has won for us in his death and resurrection. Looking back it was no doubt God's good humour that allowed the heart attack to happen not just while at the crematorium (a case, perhaps of over-identification in ministry!), but notably while saying the words: 'I am the resurrection and the life.' It was this that helped to remove fear – a verse that was no longer a text to preach on or a sentence to read out loud, but a fact to be experienced.

Catherine Marshall, writing the preface to Peter Marshall's *The First Easter* (Hodder & Stoughton, 1984) records how she first heard Peter preaching on the Easter theme at the Westminster Presbyterian Church in Atlanta. He helped the congregation to visualise the scene at the tomb of Jesus: 'A Man rises up from the cold stone slab where He had been laid. We must see Him as He walks to the threshold of the tomb, stands swaying for a moment on wounded feet and walks out into the dewy garden, alive for evermore' (p. 8). She comments:

And why was this young preacher so anxious to make this resurrection a reality to us? Why was he excited about it? He made the reason quite clear . . . Because of what had happened on that first Easter, we had a living Lord. We could each have vital communion with Him right then, tell Him our problems, get His help and direction for our lives. Moreover – and there a note of exultation came into the preacher's voice – because we could each prove Christ's aliveness for ourselves by our contact with Him, we could have the proof we needed of life after death. *Not one of us need ever fear death again.* (pp. 8–9; italics mine)

17 Must I keep giving and giving always?

'Whatever are you going to wear in Nigeria?' Molly asked, as I began packing in order to lead a university mission in Ibadan. 'You can't wear your swimming trunks!' she added, covering the embarrassment that we simply could not afford any form of proper tropical clothing suitable for preaching the gospel in. It seems ridiculous now that we should have been so short of cash. 'Well,' I said to Molly, 'we could always sell the car, then I could buy a suit.'

We were, of course, not really poor at all. We had a constant cash-flow problem, but that was because we justified to ourselves the possession of a smart modern car. 'We can't afford expensive repair bills, so it must be as new as possible,' we would argue to ourselves. 'I can't risk a late-night breakdown when I'm so busy in the Lord's work. In any case there is no time at all for the car to be off the road. Also we get a really good tax allowance if the car has a high capital value.'

With these and many other arguments we justified our actions, but we still did not have the cash for everyday purchases. Someone said that the last part of a man to get converted is his back pocket! The question of the right use of money and the right attitude to material possessions is always a difficult issue in any Christian pilgrimage, and our handling of this world's goods highlights the tension of what it means to be in the world but not of it.

The problem Molly and I found ourselves in was not just of our own making. We lived so economically in those days that we chose not to afford certain things, except on special occasions. Normal items like newspapers, bananas, orange squash or fizzy drinks were all luxuries to us. Ice creams were special treats on holiday, and holidays only happened if someone lent us a caravan free of charge. The real shortages came not so much through our mismanagement of money, but through other people's inefficiency or irresponsibility. This was notably true in the case of outside speaking engagements, when I would have spent our last pennies on petrol and the treasurer of the organisation for whom I had travelled miles to speak would either forget to offer expenses, or work them out and give exactly half the amount that the journey actually cost for petrol alone!

I would drive home from such meetings saying, 'I'm really sorry Lord to be griping in my mind about the cost of preaching the gospel. Why, we only have such a marvellous gospel of forgiveness and hope to share because you journeyed all the way from heaven to earth to die for us. You gave everything. You said yourself "Foxes have holes, and birds of the air have nests; but the Son of man has nowhere to lay his head." Lord, I am going back to a comfortable home and a loving family. We have so much compared with multitudes who are hungry and homeless. Lord we are so rich. Forgive me my mean spirit.'

I was reminded of our comparative wealth when I read some Bible study notes recently. A list of questions was given for the reader to tick off.

Have you got – tap water; walls of brick or stone; glass in your windows; a spare room; electricity or gas; a telephone within half a mile; a hospital within ten miles; a national health service; a motor vehicle; a social security system? One 'yes' means that by comparison with the majority of people in the world, you are well off. Two means that you are RICH by the world's standards; three 'yeses' means that you are very rich. Four or more that you are near the top. To say 'yes' to all ten questions means that you are very wealthy indeed.

So here we were, poor little rich people, possessing much but unable to find the ready cash to buy what was necessary for a trip to Nigeria. Then I saw exactly the right suit I needed in a small gent's outfitters in a back street in Stirchley in Birmingham. It was a sober light grey, just right for a clergyman, and it was super lightweight, just right for the heat of Nigeria. And it was reduced to £10.00 in a sale. 'That must be the one we're meant to buy,' I said to Molly. 'Maybe,' she replied, 'but what about your injections? They're another £1 5s.' In today's money that made precisely £11.25, which we didn't have. It seems quite a small amount now, but to us at that time it was a fortune. We did the only thing that Christians can do in such circumstances. We remembered how often I had taught young Christians to bring their needs to the heavenly Father, so we prayed about it.

We remembered those early lessons of prayer in our own walk with God, that we could 'cast all our anxieties on him' (cf. 1 Pet 5:7). We thought of the number of times I had preached on John 2, when Mary came to Jesus about the shortage of wine at the wedding feast. Praying the shortest prayer recorded in the Bible she said: 'They have no wine' (John 2:3). I had so often told other people that when earthly resources run out, you have only to bring the need to Jesus and he meets it super-abundantly. In this instance he provided 150 or so gallons of the best wine men had ever tasted. It was far more than Mary needed to avoid embarrassment at the feast, and it was a miraculous answer to her prayer that taught people about the new order Jesus had brought to earth. He 'manifested his glory; and his disciples believed in him' (v. 11).

Molly and I felt that we had no right to expect miraculous intervention over such a small matter. After all, we were not called to live by faith. We did have a stipend, and we could wait until the next pay day, though it was true that I had to have the jabs immediately if they were to take effect in time. Those who receive no regular salary, but who live by faith in God's provision have many dramatic stories to tell. As a young Christian I was tremendously inspired by the stories told about God's special care of the orphans in George Müller's homes in Bristol in the last century. Often Müller's faith was tested severely. The cupboard was bare and the bank balance was non-existent. But time and again the needs of the children were met to the smallest detail. Stories like that encouraged my faith, though I recognised that not every Christian is called to live like George Müller.

What I did learn from his ministry is that God is a loving father who has special care for widows and orphans. James says, 'Religion that is pure and undefiled before God and the Father is this: to visit orphans and widows in their affliction, and to keep oneself unstained from the world' (Jas 1:27). Furthermore I saw that God provided through the generous giving of Christian people. In the early church the apostles did not deal with their widows haphazardly. They urged the Christian community to choose 'seven men of good repute, full of the Spirit and of wisdom' (Acts 6:3) to deal with the practical needs of the widows. This had to be organised even though the early Spirit-filled Christians were immensely generous in helping people in need. Alongside the powerful 'testimony to the resurrection of the Lord Jesus' (Acts 4:33) there was tremendous generosity expressed within the fellowship of the church: 'There was not a needy person among them, for as many as were possessors of lands or houses sold them, and brought the proceeds of what was sold and laid it at the apostles' feet; and the distribution was made to each as any had need' (vv. 34–35).

Of course, we can argue that the world was different then, and that those were the unique days immediately following Pentecost when the Spirit of love was moving in remarkable and exceptional power to establish the new-born church. But human hearts were the same and so was human hunger. The temptation to selfishness was just the same, as we can see in the story of Ananias and Sapphira, who sold some property, as the other Christians were doing, but 'kept back some of the proceeds, and brought only a part and laid it at the apostles' feet' (Acts 5:2). Their greed led to falsehood, and Peter exposed it: 'You have not lied to men but to God' (v. 4). Falsehood led to judgment: 'When Ananias heard these words, he fell down and died' (v. 5).

We live in days when a massive worldwide industry is geared to stimulate our greed and take advantage of our selfishness. Those who can get work expect to make progress by earning more through promotion or self-advancement or at the very least through inflationary increases in salary. To move the other way, and to earn less, is a total shock to the system. I remember my own selfish thoughts when I moved from one diocese to another in the early years of my ministry. In our first curacy we earned £550 per annum, which in those days was the highest rate anywhere in the country. When we moved to another parish we had to take a considerable drop in salary. It seemed impossible that we should be able to make ends meet, at least not without a considerable change in lifestyle. I can remember feeling downcast and hard done by, resentful that other Christians in the church seemed to be doing so well when we were so hard up. It was some time before I was able to see that as a family we were blaming others for not giving more to us, when God was waiting to bless us as we learnt to give more to others. It took us so long to understand what Jesus meant when he said, 'It is more blessed to give than to receive' (Acts 20:35).

It is hard to live by this principle, as we have to survive what one writer calls 'the ever more furious orgy of consumption'. The tentacles of materialism reach out to enmesh even those who have made their protest against it. We are told that the essentially non-materialistic 'Hippies' of the Seventies have turned into the ultra-materialistic 'Yuppies' of the Eighties. Yuppies are the 'young, up and coming professionals', who have replaced their long hair-styles with short back and sides hair-cuts and have changed their flower-power carrier bags for smart business briefcases. Tents and caravans have gone as the Yuppies conform with their luxury suburban dwelling. One American Yuppie is quoted as saying, 'I've started to love the American dream. I want a business. I want to be rich. I want to have more money than I can spend. I want a Jaguar and maybe a quarter of a million dollar house.' The Yuppies' Bible has been written by Terry Cole-Whittaker: *How To Have More in a Have-Not World*.

I was appalled to find out how much Molly and I had become taken up by 'things' when we were testing out a call to serve God overseas. We had relatively few expensive possessions, but some pieces of antique furniture had been passed on to us through our families, and these were precious to us. We were only at the stage of looking at brochures of the Caribbean, thinking that we might be called to student work there, and the thought came to us about our furniture and other belongings. 'We'll have to sell it,' I said, 'it's only bits of wood, after all.' 'What, that little round table?' Molly replied, 'We've used that since the day we were married.' 'Oh, well, perhaps we could store that,' I said. 'And what about the wicker rocking-chair?' Molly asked, 'They say Winston Churchill might have used that.' The child's chair that Charis and Rachel had played with when they were small had indeed come from the home of the Duke of Marlborough. The round table had a broken foot, and the wicker chair had a broken arm, but they were precious possessions. They could become the core of a collection of antiques, we thought. We had no money with which to buy such a collection, but it was the 'in thing' to be interested in antiques.

146

We worked out the cost of storing the items we could not bring ourselves to part with, and suddenly we stopped. We looked at each other and laughed at the stupidity of our plans. We had always said that we would go anywhere in the world for the Lord. That obedience to his call meant a total renunciation of worldly possessions. 'We must live lightly to "things",' we would solemnly declare. And here we were holding back from a call to serve in another land because of a few old bits of wicker and wood! We had succumbed to the advertisers. We were trapped in materialism. We were no longer free to serve God totally. We had to repent.

No wonder Jesus told so many stories about the danger of trusting in wealth and worldly success. He knew how easy it was for the 'Hippie' of one decade to become the 'Yuppie' of the next. He told of a man who used many personal pronouns as he described his own personal ambitions and his slide into materialism:

'I will do this: I will pull down my barns, and build larger ones . . . And I will say to my soul, Soul, you have ample goods laid up for many years; take your ease, eat, drink, be merry.' But God said to him, 'Fool! This night your soul is required of you; and the things you have prepared, whose will they be?' So is he who lays up treasure for himself, and is not rich toward God. (Luke 12:18–21)

In itself, wealth is not condemned in the Bible – indeed, in Old Testament days to be wealthy was a sign of God's favour and blessing. The danger is when we love money and desire to be rich. 'He who loves money will not be satisfied with money; nor he who loves wealth, with gain: this also is vanity' (Eccl 5:10). Paul warns us against the abuse of money: 'those who desire to be rich fall into temptation, into a snare, into many senseless and hurtful desires that plunge men into ruin and destruction' (1 Tim 6:9). A writer as long ago as St John Chrysostom in the fourth century pointed out that this warning was not a word of condemnation against rich people. It is spoken to those 'who desire to be rich' and who forget that 'a man's life does not consist in the abundance of his possessions' (Luke 12:15). Jesus taught specifically that we should not lay up treasure for ourselves, but should be 'rich towards God'.

If we are journeying to heaven it is crazy to set our store on this world's wealth. Equally we cannot live in a material world without handling money and possessions. We do well to follow the advice of St Chrysostom who said, 'A man may have money and make good use of it, not over-valuing it, but bestowing it upon the poor.' To have money gives us dignity in an unequal world and is a cause for gratitude. To make good use of money means that we can not only survive in a material world but enjoy it too, as we do not over-value money, but use it. Our own sharing with the poor from our personal resources gives us integrity in challenging governments, through their elected representatives, to share food, goods and money more fairly.

It seems attractive to pull out of responsibility in our industrial society and choose a hermit-like existence of isolation from our competitive, materialistic world. The fact is we are called to own property but not to be the slaves of goods and possessions, to be wise stewards for God of good things that can be shared with those in need.

Molly and I got into a dreadful stew over this when we were preparing for marriage and were collecting things together for our new home. I was still at college with two further years of study at theological college, so we were desperately short of money. We were quite determined not to be acquisitive, or to live beyond our means, yet I can remember days when I would gaze longingly in the shop windows at Oxford, when I should have been studying, working out what items of furniture we could afford for our new home. I ended up in such turmoil about it, that all the joy was lost in building up our home. I was left with a burden of guilt about being so materialistic and about being gripped by a desire for 'things'.

This was, of course, an immature way of looking at possessions. We are material beings, living in a material world. The Bible emphasises the important place of home and family in our lives. My mean, guilty, grumbling attitude hindered the happy building up of a home through which God could express his love as we lived in partnership with him and offered hospitality to others. I was released from this miserable bondage when a clergyman preached at the wedding of two of our friends on the text: 'Unless the Lord builds the house, those who build it labour in vain' (Ps 127:1). He spoke of the joy of bringing God into all the decisions involved in building up a new home, and the way God's creating love could enable a young couple to co-operate with him in choosing and buying all the furnishings and fitments for their new home. I suddenly saw that God wanted to join in the fun of getting our home together and that he was not frowning at our modest expenditure of money on possessions.

I had quite wrongly split up material and spiritual realities in my thinking. I realised that if Jesus wants to live in me and express his love through me, my life in a material world could be given over to a spiritual purpose. As Molly and I built a home together, as we set it up, choosing wall-paper, carpets, curtains and what bits of furniture we could afford, the transforming, Christ-centred motivation was there. We could use our newly gained possessions to further God's kingdom and to express his love, providing a vehicle for growing up a believing family and offering hospitality as the Bible enjoins.

I had to discover that I did not own any of the possessions that had been causing me so much anxiety. Everything belonged to the Lord, and my responsibility was to look after his property to the best of my ability. In the Old Testament this principle was taught by the practice of tithing. The Jews had very firm instructions about the level of giving back to God from an income which was never thought to be their own, but over which each individual was appointed as a steward. One tenth of their income was for the maintenance of the Levites, the priestly tribe set aside for purposes of ministry; one tenth was for festivals and feast days; one tenth was for the poor.

As soon as we learnt about this Molly and I set aside one tenth of all our income for God's work. At first this seemed an awful lot of money, but we soon got used to the idea of living on nine-tenths of what we had formerly counted our own. Soon we became rather proud of our 'self-sacrifice' and we had a very legalistic view of tithing. Mentally we gave ourselves credit for being so well-ordered in our giving. But one day I read about John Wesley, who used to say to Christians, 'Gain all you can; save all you can; give all you can.' He lived according to these principles. In fact when his income doubled, he still lived on the same meagre amount of money and gave the rest away.

This came as a tremendous challenge to me. I suddenly realised that because Jesus had given everything for me on the cross, it was not at all generous for Molly and I to give only one tenth of our money to God's work. Indeed, it was positively mean. Furthermore, I read in the New Testament that 'God loves a cheerful giver' (2 Cor 9:7). Paul spoke of the great generosity shown by Christians in Macedonia, whose 'abundance of joy and . . . extreme poverty . . . overflowed in a wealth of liberality on their part' (2 Cor 8:2), despite their own severe test of affliction. I remembered that the left hand should not know what the right hand gives (Matt 6:3), implying that the measured out donation of the tithe which was the demand of the law should be replaced by an uncalculating generosity in giving to God's work. 'If Jesus gave everything,' I reasoned, 'how can his followers hold back anything?' Paul spoke that way: 'For you know the grace of our Lord Jesus Christ, that though he was rich, yet for your sake he became poor, so that by his poverty you might become rich' (2 Cor 8:9).

In working these things out I was greatly helped by a small booklet by Fred Mitchell entitled *The Stewardship of Money* (IVP). Fred, who was Home Director of the China Inland Mission (now the Overseas Missionary Fellowship), tells how as a small-time businessman he began to give five per cent and then ten per cent of his income. For a while he stayed at this level because, although his business prospered, the needs of his family grew at the same time. But later the profits of his business far outstripped the amount that was needed for his family, so he gave fifteen per cent, then twenty per cent, and later twenty-five per cent. He then put money aside prudently for his wife and children, so that they would not one day be a burden to others, and then, continuing in business, he gave away all his income, living economically on the interest of the capital he put by.

Fred Mitchell did not know as he took this prudent but generous course of action that he was to be taken home to God suddenly and tragically in an air crash. It was tragic for those he left, but surely he went to his reward, having laid up 'treasure in heaven' (Matt 6:20).

In his chapter on the simple life in his book *Discipleship* (Hodder & Stoughton, 1983), David Watson wrote, 'Most Christians will readily agree with teaching about faith, love, hope, service, mission. But touch the area of money, possessions and a simple lifestyle, and you will touch a very sensitive spot indeed' (p. 226). The Bible answer sounds merely pious as Paul says we are to set our hopes not 'on uncertain riches but on God who richly furnishes us with everything to enjoy' (1 Tim 6:17). But as God pours his love into our hearts by the Holy Spirit, it is a huge adjustment to find our security in his mobility, moving us on from material to spiritual desires. None of us succeeds very well in managing earthly goods in a heavenly way. However, the evidence of our hope being set on God is that we shall contribute liberally, give aid with zeal and do acts of mercy with cheerfulness (cf. Rom 12:8).

18   Keep right on . . .

When I first began the Christian life I used to worry about
whether I would be able to keep it up. I wondered if my
desire to get right with God was just another fad or
phase. I thought that it might be no more than a passing
fancy, like a boyhood fascination with collecting train
numbers or bus numbers. C. H. Spurgeon, the great
Baptist preacher, said: 'By perseverance the snail reached
the ark.' As a person I like to have instant results and
immediate success. I understand the man who prayed,
'Lord give me patience, and give it to me now.'

A verse which spoke to me many years ago rebuked
my selfish impatience. I read in 2 Peter 1:5–6, 'add to your
faith . . . patience' (AV), and I saw that to hurry things
along to suit my programme and hopes was to miss
God's timing and to doubt his sovereignty. Indeed I saw
that to lack patience was to lack perseverance, an essential mark of anyone committed to following the pattern
set by Jesus Christ. Paul prayed, 'May the Lord direct
your hearts to the love of God and to the steadfastness (or
patience) of Christ' (2 Thess 3:5). This involves both
patiently waiting for Christ and also finding the patience
in our experience which is the gift of Christ to our lives.
James 1:4 says that patience perfects Christian character;
as it is modelled on Jesus our example, the one who is 'the
pioneer and perfecter of our faith, who for the joy that
was set before him endured the cross, despising the
shame, and is seated at the right hand of the throne of
God' (Heb 12:2).

I feared that I might grow out of this interest in

'religion' as I had grown out of other teenage hobbies. What I had not realised at that stage was that we fill our time with hobbies and pastimes because of an inner need for fulfilment or recognition. It's part of our creative instinct and often develops the competitive element in our natures, as we try to achieve the highest possible standard in our chosen sphere. So there is a link between our normal human instincts for purposeful, creative activity and the ultimate fulfilment of our purpose as human beings, to be related to God, with sins forgiven, through faith in Jesus Christ. The difference is that in our hobbies we strive hard, but always fall short of a perfect standard, whether it is in music, art, sport or collecting stamps. There is always more to achieve.

What we know from the Bible is that absolute perfection lies at the end of the road, once God's Holy Spirit comes into our lives. His work is to make us like Jesus. He helps us to walk free from our sin so that it no longer dominates our experience. 'Sin will have no dominion over you, since you are not under law but under grace,' Paul writes (Rom 6:14). 'Now that you have been set free from sin and have become slaves of God, the return you get is sanctification and its end, eternal life' (Rom 6:22). In 2 Corinthians 3:17–18 Paul attributes this working of God to change the human heart to the Holy Spirit: 'Now the Lord is the Spirit, and where the Spirit of the Lord is, there is freedom. And we all, with unveiled face, beholding the glory of the Lord, are being changed into his likeness from one degree of glory to another; for this comes from the Lord who is the Spirit.'

It is not that we are perfectly free from sin in our journey through life this side of the grave. A young fellow, Peter, who was in our youth group when I worked at Birmingham Cathedral, got in with a crowd of Christians who taught just that. They said that as soon as you turn to Christ for forgiveness and believe that he died on the cross for all your past sins, and as soon as God's Holy Spirit comes and completely fills your life, you have arrived at a state of sinless perfection. You can no longer do wrong. I asked him, 'What does your Mum think about you, or your best friend, or your employer?' He had no answer. He knew that he and his misguided Christian friends, who were prepared to overlook his extreme selfishness and pride, were the only ones who would dare to make such a bold claim.

The perfection that the Bible promises comes when we are fully like Christ, with a risen body, beyond the grave, in the beauty of heaven. It is God who promises to get us there.

I was preaching in a church in Helsinki during an overseas tour with our church choir, when a man came up to me after the service to say how God had spoken to him during our visit. I gave him a small booklet called *Open to God*, which describes some of the things that God has done for us in our church in Harborne, and inside the front cover I wrote out the verse which had meant so much to me in the early days of my Christian life: 'I am sure that he who began a good work in you will bring it to completion at the day of Jesus Christ' (Phil 1:6). The man was a Russian colonel, staying with friends in Finland, and through an interpreter with tears in his eyes, he acknowledged that he had grasped the truth of that verse. He saw that his encounter with the gospel of Christ would not be a flash in the pan, because God would take charge of his life and take him through to the ultimate perfection of the day of Jesus Christ.

Now that thirty-three years have passed since I was brought to faith in Christ, I laugh at my own early insecurities and doubts. I realise now that in those first days of faith when I wondered if the experience of God would last, or whether I could keep up my side of the bargain I had made with Jesus, I was just like God's people in the Old Testament when they failed to trust God in the difficult times they encountered in the wilderness. They grumbled at him when they ran short of water and food, as we have already seen. 'He made streams come out of the rock, and caused waters to flow down like rivers. Yet they sinned still more against him' (Ps 78:16–17). And what provoked God's anger against their disobedience was that 'they had no faith in God, and did not trust his saving power' (v. 22).

I was the same. As a young Christian I would deliberately go against God during the daytime, and then wonder why I was so out of sorts, without any real trust in God, during my evening prayer time. I got to the point of packing up my prayers because I felt so ashamed of my wrong-doing, and found myself blaming God for what was entirely my failure. I came near the point of wondering if this experiment with Christianity was indeed going to be like one of those childhood hobbies – something that was started enthusiastically, but never persevered with. When I was a boy I used to revive some of my hobbies when I was ill in bed. By contrast I found that in my walk with Christ, it was when I was spiritually unwell that I was tempted to give up my calling. However, secretly I despised those who began things and did not have the determination to complete them. I did not want to be like my sisters who had drawers full of uncompleted bits of knitting and half-made dresses. I was always disappointed at my own tendency to take up new interests, and then to drop them.

I could not grasp at the time that perseverance in the Christian life was guaranteed by God and not by my endeavour. As a new Christian I was often helped to understand the deepest truths of God by the simplest illustration, and although I found it hard to grasp what some of the old Puritan writers meant when they wrote in very learned terms about 'the perseverance of the saints', I found it very easy to follow a story told by one of the many Bible teachers who gave us instruction as young Christians. He told the story of some boys at a Christian summer camp by the seaside who were helped to put their faith in Christ for the first time.

One of the lads spoke to the camp leader about the

problems he felt he would have when he went home, because his family were not believers. He wondered if he could keep up his new Christian life away from the friendship and support of the camp. The leader did not answer his question, but said, 'Reach out and hold my hand as tightly as you can.' The small boy did so, but as the leader pulled his hand away hard, he could not keep his grip on it. The man was far too strong for the boy's small fingers. In fact the lad fell backwards to the ground. When he had picked himself up, the boy was asked to reach out his hand again. 'Now let me hold your hand,' the leader said. This time the boy pulled and struggled to get free, but he could not succeed. The man's strong grasp held him tight.

The lesson was obvious – to me, at least. From a simple picture I was given a new trust in a loving God who would never let go of me. It helped me to believe in God's good purpose of rescuing and forgiving us through the obedience of Jesus in taking away our sins and dying our death on the cross, and then coming alive to be a friend and companion in the Christian pilgrimage. The added bonus of the gift of his Holy Spirit to keep us from sinning more and more was a further dimension of security that I was only just beginning to grasp.

Later on in Christian ministry, when I was working among university students, I became puzzled about how to counsel those who claimed once to have been Christians, but had fallen right away from Christ and seemingly had no faith at all. Should I correct what I felt to be their misunderstanding, and say, 'Well, of course, when you were younger, you "believed in vain" (1 Cor 15:2). It was never a genuine experience of God. If there had been any real evidence of new life in Christ, you would still be trusting him today. After all, once he has you in his grasp he will never let you go. Jesus said, "no one shall snatch them [his 'sheep'] out of my hand" (John 10:28).' That seemed a very straight, if somewhat glib, analysis of the predicament of these students. But I did not want them to doubt what might have been a very genuine childhood experience which should be built on – not knocked down. Should I not rather say, 'Let's be careful about what you are saying. You might have had a very sincere and genuine turning to God, but the experience has grown cold on you. You have gone into a dark tunnel of doubt and can hardly see the light at the other end. It does not mean you are not still on the journey. Or, to change the picture, you are like a hibernating hedgehog. You look, read and feel nothing, but hearing the gospel today has caused you to put up one or two of your prickles. That is surely an evidence of life!'

I puzzled over what advice to give in such cases. The problem was solved for me when John Stott called by at our house in London on the way to a prayer meeting. It was just a friendly call, but I took the opportunity to 'talk shop' and to share this difficulty.

'The answer is simple,' he said, 'it does not matter if the original experience was a true encounter with Christ or a false start. The fact is, either way, such a student is in the far country of sin, cut off from God, and like the lost boy in the story that Jesus told, the only thing to do is repent. When he finally came to the end of himself, and realised that he could not survive alone, the young man said: "I will arise and go to my father, and I will say to him, 'Father, I have sinned against heaven and before you; I am no longer worthy to be called your son . . .'" (Luke 15:18–19). Whether the person you are talking to has ever truly repented before, he or she must do so today.'

'But which do you think is the most likely analysis of their condition?' I asked, still pressing the point. 'The normal characteristic of a Christian is to go on with God,' John replied. 'If a person does not persevere, you have cause to doubt the genuineness of their first profession of faith.' He then quoted from Colossians 1:21 onwards, where Paul informs his readers of all that Christ has done for them, despite the fact that they 'once were estranged and hostile in mind': 'he has now reconciled you in his body of flesh by his death, in order to present you holy. and blameless and irreproachable before him, *provided'* (and in his tone of voice John laid great emphasis on this conditional word) *'provided* that you continue in the faith, stable and steadfast, not shifting from the hope of the gospel which you heard' (vv. 22–23).

I should have known this before, but it just had not dawned. Because the Christian life is a matter of moment by moment repenting and believing, it is clear that the conditions of obedience to God's word are constantly necessary for proper growth. The students I had been speaking to had clearly tried to grasp God's hand in their own strength, and they had not sustained a life of love and devotion, praying daily to him, and listening to his word and applying it to their lives in regular Bible study. Clearly they had lost all joy in worship, and they were as bankrupt spiritually as the 'prodigal son' was literally in the far country away from his father.

From then on I often said to people who were on the brink of faith in Christ, 'I cannot help you to believe. I cannot clear up all your doubts. But I can help you to repent. If you are willing to make the journey home to your heavenly Father, and make a new start with him, through faith in Christ, then you will be journeying on the road of obedience, trust and perseverance. The key thing is not to waste time querying your past experience and trying to interpret it. You must turn back to God now – repent now. It's so easy if sin is forsaken, because in the story Jesus told, the Father who had been so badly wronged by his son was already running to greet him and welcome him home. When we turn to God in repentance and start obeying his word to us, we find a similar welcome and a real experience of God's working in our lives.'

The other major query I have always had about keeping on to the end of the road with God concerns the matter of persecution. Many Christians in the Western world have a very easy road to travel. We are not taken hostage or put in prison for our faith. We don't have to make decisions about not compromising our faith in front of hostile witnesses. And yet today there are thousands in prison for Christ all over the world. Only a few of them hit the headlines of the Christian press, let alone the national media. I used to feel so weak and frail as a Christian that I was quite sure I would be the first to deny Christ under the pressure of persecution. I was truly anxious lest I should end up by committing apostasy or being disloyal to Christ.

My fears were helped by meeting two modern-day confessors of the faith. One was Pastor Richard Wurmbrand, who came to preach for us on more than one occasion when I was on the staff of Birmingham Cathedral. As a Rumanian pastor he was imprisoned for his faith for fourteen years by communists. As he preached in the cathedral he suddenly let out a blood-curdling cry. He said, 'That's the cry of those who suffer in prison for Christ's sake. Where are your cries and prayers for them? They pray every day for you.' I was made deeply aware of how little we identify with our brothers and sisters in prison. The New Testament is quite clear about our responsibility in this matter. We have a special care for 'prisoners and captives'. Jesus gave them a special place in his outline of the Messiah's ministry, quoting from the prophet Isaiah: 'He has sent me to proclaim release to the captives and recovering of sight to the blind, to set at liberty those who are oppressed' (Luke 4:18).

But what really impressed me about Pastor Wurmbrand was the victory of his person. It hardly seemed possible that he had been tortured for his faith. He only spoke of love for his captors. He said of the suffering of fellow believers, 'I have seen Christians in communist prisons with 50 lb of chains on their feet, tortured with red-hot pokers, in whose throats spoonfuls of salt have been forced, being kept afterwards without water, starving, whipped, suffering from cold, and praying with fervour for the communists. It is humanly inexplicable.'

Suddenly I saw it. What is 'humanly inexplicable' is possible with God. This was his gift of love – a special outpouring that none of us could know until we were in the place of persecution. I realised that even through suffering and trial God would keep me. Though I could only measure my extreme weakness and fear in facing even the thought of such testing, he would give a miraculous measure of grace in order to cope with it. Peter promised it: 'If you are reproached for the name of Christ, you are blessed, because the spirit of glory and of God rests upon you . . . Therefore let those who suffer according to God's will do right and entrust their souls to a faithful Creator' (1 Pet 4:14, 19).

The other notable confessor of the faith, whom I knew during his last years as Bishop of Birmingham, was Leonard Wilson, a man much loved by those who served under him. During the Second World War he was Bishop of Singapore and was taken prisoner by the Japanese. At his last diocesan clergy conference before he retired, Bishop Wilson spoke movingly of his experiences in prison. He spoke of how he prayed for courage, but was almost afraid to, lest he should suffer yet more hours of 'ignoble pain'. He told of how four soldiers were beating him repeatedly with rubber truncheons as he was under interrogation. They asked, 'Do you still believe in God?' With God's help he was able to reply, 'Yes, I do.' Then they asked, 'Why does God not save you?' Again he replied, 'God does save me,' admitting that he was able to say this only by the help of the Holy Spirit. He shared with his captors that the victory and salvation of God was experienced not in deliverance from suffering, but in giving him the Spirit to bear it. He felt it was verging on blasphemy to pray the actual words that Jesus prayed on the cross, forgiving his enemies, but he repeatedly prayed, 'Help them to see that I am innocent.'

Then Bishop Wilson was given a marvellous vision from God. He was able to see his torturers not as they were but as they had been. Once they were little children playing with their brothers and sisters, and happy in their parents' love. Seeing them like this he found that he could love them even as they brought him pain and punishment. Though he was not called at that time to make the ultimate sacrifice, Leonard Wilson showed remarkable steadfastness and endurance under fierce provocation. He kept right on to the end, and ultimately had the unusual privilege of confirming the chief of his torturers.

When we find it hard to live with others, or when it is difficult even to accept ourselves, it is a true gift from God to be able to see that we are like little children in his sight. Of course, some children can be cruel. Sin spoils us from the moment we are born. But children can have a simple trust, a sense of innocence and an unquestioning willingness to grow and learn and achieve. Jesus said, 'Truly, I say to you, whoever does not receive the kingdom of God like a child shall not enter it' (Mark 10:15). Childlike trust in the Father's love keeps our hand in his. However hard the road – and for some it can mean imprisonment or persecution, or for others the more everyday suffering of rejection, illness or loss of a loved one – he will keep us, as we trust him, until our last day on earth and beyond. 'He has said, "I will never fail you nor forsake you." Hence we can confidently say, "The Lord is my helper, I will not be afraid; what can man do to me?"' (Heb 13:5–6).

19 . . . to the end of the road

It seems hard to end on a theme of perseverance, suffering and trial, even though these things are the inevitable ingredients of Christian pilgrimage here on earth. The story so far has focused on the personal walk that each one of us can have with God as we put our faith in Jesus Christ for the forgiveness of our sins and for a new way of life. As Christians we are called to narrate what 'we have seen and heard' of God in Christ (1 John 1:3) so that others can be helped.

But behind the simple personal story, big themes are touched – matters relating to sickness, suffering, death and conflicting ideologies. The Christian who tries to walk alone with God in an isolated pietism, a private devotion, a personalised independence from others is a living contradiction of the gospel of Christ, which speaks of us living out the new life in relationship with others in the church. The New Testament describes a fellowship of people, what Peter called 'a chosen race, a royal priesthood, a holy nation, God's own people' (1 Pet 2:9). To keep on to the end means that I must have the prayers and love and fellowship of God's people, as well as fulfilling the personal conditions of repentance and obedience in a personal relationship with God.

The oldest and simplest illustration of this principle, found in many books of talks for Sunday school children, describes a preacher taking a box of matches out of his pocket. Taking one match out of the box, he held it up to show how easily it could be broken. Snap! The match was in two pieces. Then he took some twenty or thirty matches, held them tightly together, and tried to break them in two. Of course, he couldn't. He showed that we are strong as long we are together in the fellowship of the church. One Christian alone is easily tempted and broken; several together can readily encourage each other with God's promises and with prayer.

But the church is not *just* a collection of Christians. It is meant to be a living organism. Paul calls it 'the body of Christ' (1 Cor 12:27). In our pilgrimage through life we are, as members of Christ's body, to 'grow up in every way into him who is the head, into Christ, from whom the whole body, joined and knit together by every joint with which it is supplied, when each part is working properly, makes bodily growth and upbuilds itself in love' (Eph 4:15–16). As Christ's body on earth, we witness not only to the possibility of a personal relationship with God, but to his justice and righteousness, and to his holiness.

Jesus said to his disciples, 'You are the salt of the earth' (Matt 5:13). We must be a preserving agent in society, to keep the world from corrupting because of its evil choices. One individual alone cannot achieve much, but a company of Christians can take a stand on a moral issue, and through proper processes get the law applied or even get it changed and strengthened.

Mary Whitehouse has often been made out by media people to be a figure of fun, but deep down many respect her enormously for taking such a bold stand for Christian standards, particularly in relation to television programmes. I remember taking part in a radio interview following a court case in which Mary had been involved as a witness. The journalist who was to interview me live in the studio and Mary on the telephone was literally quaking with fear not only because of her professional competence in such interviews, but because of her spiritual power. She could not have succeeded alone. She needed other Christians to pray for her and back her in that witness, to be salt in the earth, preventing any further decline in standards.

There are many other public issues on which Christians can unite to highlight the problems of injustice and poverty in society. The Archbishop of Canterbury's report *Faith in the City* came as a shaft of light to show us the appalling circumstances of many who live in urban priority areas. Not everyone welcomed the light, and progress in improving people's circumstances has been slow. But at least some light has been shone into some very unsatisfactory corners of contemporary city life.

Jesus said, 'You are the light of the world' (Matt 5:14). Christ's body on earth is increasingly aware of its call to shine, as light, in darkness. This is the public purpose that unites all the private pilgrimages of individual believers, and for it to happen we must be committed to the life of a local church. Only then can we fulfil the task Jesus gave to the body of disciples – 'As the Father has sent me, even so I send you' (John 20:21).

But though it is the call of God's people to make his world a better place, many centuries of witness to God's love in Christ have achieved little improvement. We have developed technically, but wars, terrorism, disease and disaster still plague us all. Jesus in fact promised a worsening of circumstances before the end of the world comes: 'For in those days there will be such tribulation as has not been from the beginning of creation which God created until now, and never will be' (Mark 13:19). Paul was similarly pessimistic about the last days:

. . . in the last days there will come times of stress. For men will be lovers of self, lovers of money, proud, arrogant, abusive, disobedient to their parents, ungrateful, unholy, inhuman, implacable, slanderers, profligates, fierce, haters of good, treacherous, reckless, swollen with conceit, lovers of pleasure rather than lovers of God, holding the form of religion but denying the power of it. (2 Tim 3:1–5)

Fortunately, the future is not in our hands, but in God's. He is the God of the new happening and of a future hope beyond this world's experience. He said, 'Behold, I am doing a new thing' (Isa 43:19); 'A new spirit I will put within you' (Ezek 36:26). Jesus said, 'A new commandment I give to you, that you love one another; even as I have loved you, that you also love one another' (John 13:34). People noticed a new authority in Jesus as he taught with signs and wonders. After Pentecost they saw the same power in Christians in the church. Jesus had, after all, promised 'greater works than these will [you] do' (John 14:12). As Jesus came with new wine to stretch the old religion's wine skins, he came with new doctrine to stretch the people's minds. He promised the new birth we have spoken about in these chapters, and from his new creation we form the new loving community of people on earth, who are being fitted for a new world as we wait on tip-toe for the 'the new heavens and the new earth'. Already 'he puts a new song in our mouths' (Ps 40:3) and in heaven there will be 'a new song before the throne' (Rev 14:3).

One day everything that we have shared together will be history – events and happenings, past and done. Together with tears, mourning, crying, pain, and even death itself, this story of pilgrimage will be part of 'the former things' that 'have passed away' (Rev 21:4). The one thing we can have on earth which will be at the centre of heaven's life is Jesus himself. The new city 'has no need of sun or moon to shine upon it, for the glory of God is its light, and its lamp is the Lamb' (Rev 21:23). He will be everything then. We can make him everything now.

THE RENEWAL OF THE MIND

Mike Pratt

Even when people come to a living faith in Jesus Christ, they carry with them assumptions, attitudes and patterns of thought that are shaped by an increasingly secular world. If Christians are to live transformed lives, and if God is to transform western culture, the mind must be challenged and changed by the Holy Spirit.

Mike Pratt, in this stimulating and practical book, explores this theme in depth, writing in a lively and popular style which will enable many to understand and apply this vital teaching. Repentance has an important place in the Holy Spirit's work of renewal, and the meaning and excitement of true repentance is drawn out. The author explains some of the stages as faith matures, and shares from his own experience what 'renewal of the mind' means in practice, and how it can transform not only the mind, but the whole of life and ministry. Finally, he shows how Christians can hold fast to what God has done, and not slide back into old ways of thinking. This book will help all, both individuals and churches, who wish to 'keep in step with the Spirit'.

The Revd Mike Pratt is Area Dean of Harrow, and Vicar of St Andrew's, Roxbourne.

MONEY, SEX AND POWER

Richard Foster

'Compulsive reading of a far higher literary quality than any other modern Christian book. It deserves to become a classic of modern spirituality.'

Christian Weekly Newspapers

Richard J. Foster, author of the bestselling *Celebration of Discipline* has done it again. He now turns from a devotional to an ethical perspective and looks with characteristic warmth and insight at the three issues of money, sex and power. He asserts that 'no issues touch us more profoundly or universally. No topics cause more controversy. No human realities have greater power to bless or curse. No three things have been more sought after or are more in need of a Christian response.'

In *Money, Sex and Power*, Richard J. Foster discerns those biblical principles which enable us to live out a truly Christian response that is both appropriate for modern society and authentically Christian.

'Altogether, a most compassionate and articulate guide to these significant areas of Christian living.'

On Being (Australia) June 87